Conflict Analysis

NEW SCIENCE SERIES

General Editor
SIR GRAHAM SUTTON, C.B.E., D.Sc., LL.D., F.R.S.

Conflict Analysis

Michael Nicholson

Director; Richardson Institute
for Conflict and Peace Research, London

The English Universities Press Limited

To my first wife

ISBN 0 340 12484 9 Boards
ISBN 0 340 11783 4 Paper

First published 1970

The English Universities Press Ltd
St Paul's House, Warwick Lane, London EC4M 7BT

Printed and bound in Great Britain by
W & J Mackay & Co Ltd Chatham

Editor's Foreword

The aim of the New Science Series is to provide authoritative accounts of topics chosen from the wide range of modern science. The series includes books by experts in the physical, biological and social sciences. In the selection of titles and in the treatment, the needs of the reader who has a lively curiosity about the world around him, and is prepared to make a conscious effort to understand the thoughts and achievements of specialists, have been kept to the fore. Although special attention has been given to the younger generation, it is hoped that the series will also be of interest and value to more mature minds.

These books have been written to attract a wide audience. In an age in which life is increasingly affected by scientific discovery it seems essential that the practitioners should endeavour to make clear, in part if not in whole, the aims and implications of their work. It is hoped that the New Science Series will make a contribution to this end.

O.G.S.

Preface

I have written this book to describe to the general reader current work on the application of the methods and tools of the social sciences to further the understanding and to promote an ultimate cure of violent and, in particular, international conflict. In a new discipline, the selection of topics and the emphasis given to them is more the victim of personal idiosyncrasy than in more established fields. However, I have not been wilfully perverse in these matters and I hope that at least some of the workers in the field will agree that my discussions of the discipline have not been too bizarre.

The book was largely written whilst I was Senior Research Fellow in Conflict Studies at the University of Lancaster and completed whilst I was a staff member of the Centre for the Analysis of Conflict, University College, London. I am grateful to Professor Philip Reynolds of the former, to Dr. John Burton of the latter and to my other colleagues for their tolerance. I could mention many names, but shall restrict myself to my former graduate students David Chapman, Gordon Hilton, Robin Jenkins, John Macrae, Paul Smoker and David Wilkinson. The list is, perhaps, archaic as their names are now widely known in the field of conflict research.

The Richardson Institute for Conflict and Peace Research, my present professional home, is called after Lewis Fry Richardson, whose work is discussed in this book. The Institute's function is to carry on research into the sort of topic discussed in this book and, hopefully, in such a way that the book will become out of date quickly. The importance I attribute to Richardson as a founder of the field is, I think, a just appraisal, and is without hagiographic intent.

By tradition, wives come at the end of prefaces. I cannot say that, without mine, I would not have been able to write a book on this subject. I probably would. However, it would have been a different book—inferior and narrower in scope. For helping me to avoid this, I am grateful to her.

Contents

Contents

chapter one

Social Science and the Study of Conflict

1 Peace and War

War is one of mankind's favourite occupations. As far back as we can tell, men have devoted the best of their minds and bodies to the problem of killing other men. This still persists. Man is the only animal which takes the business of killing other members of his species with such seriousness. Other primates kill the members of other species, usually for food. Members of the same species also often fight amongst themselves for mates, territory and so on, but only rarely do they fight to the death. Killing amongst the non-human primates is equivalent more to murder than to war. War is a predominantly human activity[1].*

Despite its frequency, war is an activity which conflicts with the aims of most other human activities, such as the quest for wealth, knowledge, a happy family life and so on, all of which are much better carried on under conditions of peace. The paradox is apparent.

War is not universally abhorred. People's attitudes towards violence culminating in death and suffering are ambivalent, combining horror for its obvious miseries with fascination for its splendour and the opportunities for gallantry and even for a noble death which war provides. Attitudes to war during the twentieth century seem to have altered somewhat, and common belief seems to regard war as a regrettable necessity rather than as something desirable in itself. The vast slaughter of the First World War may have had something to do with this. Perhaps more important is our greater belief in the prospects of controlling society. War at one time was regarded as inevitable. However, so was slavery, which is now an almost defunct institution. If war is not seen to be an inevitable feature of human life, dislike of it will make people work to stop it rather than make the best of a bad job. Despite the change in attitudes, we seem today to have had very little success in stopping wars being fought. Frequently, nations or societies get into positions where, to many people, the only way out seems to be to fight. Why should this be?

* Figures in square brackets refer to the list of References on p. 164.

Conflict Analysis or Conflict Studies is based on the notion that we cannot answer the question 'How can war be stopped?' without going back to the question 'Why are wars fought?' The second will not give an automatic answer to the first, but it is a necessary prerequisite. It is the second of these questions which Conflict Analysis, as a discipline, is trying to answer. The discipline is still at a very elementary stage, and the first crude results are just appearing. This book is a description of some of the more promising lines of enquiry. In some chapters the emphasis is on the methods of enquiry—such as the discussion of gaming and simulation—and in some chapters the emphasis is on the substantive problem as in the chapters on International Crises or Arms Races. All are designed to give a picture of the discipline which is advancing both in its methodological and substantive aspects and the two cannot properly be separated. The patchwork quilt effect which may emerge from the book also mirrors the diversity of the lines of enquiry within the discipline.

2 The Definition of Conflict

This book as a whole is primarily concerned with international conflicts, and in particular with conflicts which erupt or may erupt into violence. However, conflict is a general feature of human activity and it is towards its more general aspects that we will turn for the moment.

A conflict exists when two people wish to carry out acts which are mutually inconsistent. They may both want to do the same thing, such as eat the same apple, or they may want to do different things where the different things are mutually incompatible, such as when they both want to stay together but one wants to go to the cinema and the other stay at home. A conflict is resolved when some mutually consistent set of actions is worked out. The definition of conflict can be extended from single people to groups (such as nations), and more than two parties can be involved in the conflict. The principles remain the same.

Conflict is defined as an activity which takes places between sentient, though not necessarily rational beings. If two astronomical bodies collide we do not say that they are in conflict. Therefore a conflict must be defined in terms of the wants or needs of the parties involved. For example, there is a more or less permanent conflict over Berlin between the various powers who feel they have an interest in it. This conflict comes about through the perceived structure of what the powers want. The conflict could end if the powers' wants altered. Thus there is no conflict between Iceland and the Soviet Union over the status of Berlin.

Although in one sense conflicts may be subjective, what a person (or a nation) wants is an objective characteristic of that person. Wants are subjective in the sense that an answer to the question 'Why do you want to do X?' can be given only in terms either of 'Because I want to do Y and X is the means of achieving it' or 'I ought to do X' (where X may be something basic like stay alive—it is nevertheless a want). Finally, having gone through a chain of reasons, all given in terms of either wants or obligations, one ends up with a statement of the type 'Just because I want to' or 'Just because I ought to'. There is no external justification for these final statements of wants. Thus, the desires of a nation (more strictly its decision-makers) which motivate its actions are based ultimately on needs or obligations (which might cynically be regarded as rationalised needs), but these sets of needs and obligations are justifiable only within their own self-contained system. In this sense they are subjective. The desires of, say, the West German government concerning the situation in Berlin can be justified only in terms of other desires, or obligations. However, the aims of the West German decision-makers concerning Berlin are an objective, though not thereby an unalterable, characteristic which they possess and are thus quite 'real' as far as the analysis of behaviour is concerned.

Conflicts abound in all forms of social behaviour. In industry there are strikes, in international politics there are wars and threats of wars, in marriages there are quarrels, and, when people tire of acting out their conflicts in these fields, they can always turn to sport as a highly institutionalised and constrained form of conflict. While these forms of conflict are very different from each other, they are all recognised as conflicts and hence have some common attributes. It is thus legitimate to look at conflict as a general form of conduct to see what insights are to be gained from looking at the activity as a whole. There may be none, but the likelihood is that there will be. Though our interest is primarily in war and its causes, the more general analysis involving an analysis of some other forms of conflict will help provide, if nothing else, a set of concepts which will be of use in tackling the prime problem. Indeed it is arguable that the best way of understanding international conflict is by the indirect route of examining other forms of conflict and then using the insights so obtained to examine the causes of war.

Suppose we look at a question such as bargaining. Bargaining in general is a process whereby two (or more) parties, whose aims at least partially conflict, endeavour to find some mutually satisfactory agreement which will enable them to proceed in harmony. Consider a trade union and a firm bargaining over the wage rate. The union want the highest rate possible and the management want the lowest. Both start off the bargaining with demands

3

which are incompatible with each other and then bargain until they reach a level which both will accept and which is normally in between the two original starting-points. It is not just a matter of talking, however. If the management appear recalcitrant, the union can call a strike. The firm can have a lock-out. This, however, is relatively infrequent these days, but not because the managements have a stronger social conscience than the unions. The bargaining situation is asymmetrical and in the employer's favour. The firm makes the positive act of handing out the wages—the workers are involved only in the passive act of receiving them. The union cannot directly force the management to hand out a higher wage and, prior to an agreement, the situation always heavily favours the employer. The union can break this *status quo* position only by calling the strike. Thus, as the situation of non-agreement favours the employers, it is natural that the hostilities in an industrial dispute should normally be initiated by the union. The strike will end at some time either with a concession by one or the other party or, most commonly, some concessions on both sides.

Now this situation has some parallels with international conflicts. Suppose two nations disagree over the degree of influence which they will both exert over some area. They might discuss the problem and conceivably arrive directly at some solution. In the bargaining, however, the prospect of fighting will come up, and indeed the situation might break out into war. The war may end by the submission of one party or some agreement.

There are some analogies between the two processes of industrial and international disagreement. The goals of the parties are initially incompatible, and the process of bargaining is to make them compatible. In both cases, there is the possibility of indulging in some mutually harmful activity so as to force the rival to accept some otherwise unacceptable solution—in the industrial case the strike, and in the international case the war. An analysis of the industrial bargain might conceivably suggest hints for the analysis of the international bargain. It is not difficult to spot breakdowns in the analogy, and the most such a procedure can do is suggest ways of going about the prime problem. But this is by no means a trivial contribution.

Perhaps the most serious way in which the analogy breaks down is with respect to the issue of violence. Most strikes today do not involve violence, whereas war, by definition, is a violent act. Even in the days and places where strikes often were accompanied by violence, the violence was not the primary element in the conflict. The threat of the strike to the employers was primarily the withdrawal of the work force, not the possibility of riots.

Now our attitudes to violence are curious and, as remarked earlier, by no means completely consistent. When wars break out it is not infrequent for the

4

populations of the warring states to get violently enthusiastic. The suggestion of negotiation becomes the suggestion of treason. The only acceptable alternative for each opponent is the complete subjection of the other. Even in more limited wars, victory in the limited sense becomes the requirement. This is not true in the non-violent conflict. Even in the midst of the strike, negotiation is a proper activity and a solution involving a compromise is acceptable.

3 The Nature of the Social Sciences

The social sciences are the study of the actions of people in relation to other people. Economics, social psychology, anthropology are all examples of social sciences. Psychology is on the borderline in that, while it deals with the behaviour of people, it is often concerned with them on their own. That is, the interaction of decisions which is such a conspicuous element in the other social sciences is not a feature of the study of at least large areas of psychology. However, the methodological problems and techniques of psychology have much in common with some, at least, of the other social sciences and for our purposes we can consider them together.

The social sciences claim to be sciences and thus have two characteristics. First, there are propositions which apply to classes of events, and not only to individual events. The aim is to formulate theories of behaviour and events. The second characteristic is that these theories should be testable and that there should be some general, if possibly rough, agreement amongst the practitioners concerning what is an appropriate test. This means that when a theory is postulated it must be phrased in such a form that, when we examine the data from the real world, we can establish whether the data are consistent or inconsistent with the theory. This is, of course, tied up with the social scientists's first aim of generalisation. There is not a great deal of point in elaborating theories if one cannot tell whether they are consistent with the facts or not.

A common method in both the social and natural sciences is known by the cumbrous name of the *hypothetico-deductive method*. The procedure consists of assuming, for the sake of argument, the truth of a few hypotheses about the state of the world and then following through the logical implications of these hypotheses. There then emerges a broader set of interrelated self-consistent propositions. However, a set of self-consistent propositions is not the same as a set of correct propositions about the world, and the theory, as the set of propositions can be referred to, must be tested against empirical reality, there being many ways in which this can be done. If it fails the tests, then the theory must be scrapped, but if it passes the tests and is not refuted by them, it can be provisionally accepted as a 'true' theory, that is, one which explains the facts and, if sufficiently developed, can predict. The more tests the theory passes, the greater is the confidence with which the theory can be held. No theory is 'proved' true, though in the case of some physical theories, such as that the planets revolve round the sun, the doubt is rather technical.

Theories which evolve from the hypothetico-deductive method rarely appear as testable theories very quickly. There is a long period of incubation which precedes this, as theories often are derived from extremely simple frameworks which either describe nothing at all which appears in the real world, or things which could appear only under very artificial experimental circumstances. The logical implications of such simple preliminary theories or 'models' are often explored, as in the case of many economic models, in very great detail. Alternatively they can be explored experimentally as is the case with the Prisoners' Dilemma, a construction which is discussed in some detail later in the book. The purpose of such simple models is that they are usually prerequisites of a full-scale theory in cases where the theory concerns very complex structures. Sometimes the purpose of the models is to lay bare the logical nature of the situation under examination, when this would be impossible in the more complex real-life situation. An appreciation of the fundamental logical characteristics of some phenomena can be of direct help in understanding the reality. However, it is also the case that the simple model can be the base on which a more complex model is built. Having understood the operations of the simple structure, it becomes easier to tag on the more and more complications which bring it nearer to reality and thus to being a genuinely testable theory. To criticise simple and sometimes blatantly unrealistic theories for their oversimplicity alone is merely to criticise them for not being complete. The process of completing them may be a long one requiring the contributions of many people. For theories of most social processes, close correspondences with reality can hardly be expected overnight.

We can categorise this in the diagram below.

The top half of the diagram labelled 'theory' illustrates the processes of theory development. On the left-hand side we have the hypothetico-deductive method as used to construct simple models or theories of artificial worlds. The models start with the assumptions, work to the deductions which can be made from these assumptions, and the combined set of propositions is the model. On the right-hand side is a similar framework for the theory proper. This is a theory of the real world. In structure it is the same. There are a set of assumptions, a set of implications deduced from these assumptions and together these form the body of the theory.

The theory of the real world can be tested against evidence from the real world. Indeed, if it cannot, then it does not qualify as a theory, as understood scientifically. This does not mean that every single proposition in the theory is necessarily testable. It merely means that sufficient of this theory is testable such that the non-testable parts are implications of the testable parts. The theories of the simplified world are not testable in the same way. As they are

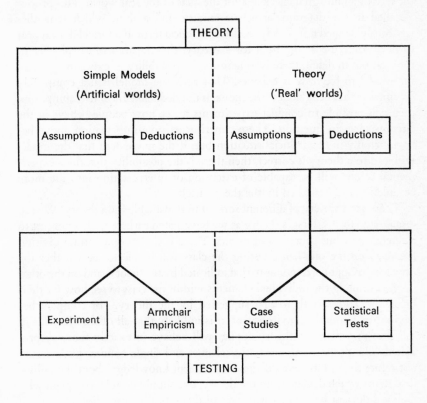

Figure 1.1

not intended as explanations of the real world, direct testing against the real world is an irrelevant activity.

However, the simple models are not independent of reality. There are criteria other than internal logical consistency by which we can evaluate models, at least provisionally. A model is a step towards a theory. Its immediate practical use may be simply to isolate the basic structure of a problem so that more insight can be gained into the behaviour of the real world even before a theory in any strict sense has been formulated. However, it can be used in this way only if, by suitable elaboration, it holds out some hope of being extended into a theory. Formal criteria for assessing whether a model is likely to lead to a fruitful theory are hard to establish. There is just the subjective judgement about whether the model appears to make sense or not in the face of an informal check against the facts of the real world. This process is called in the diagram 'armchair empiricism', a term which is neither rigorously defined nor widely used as a technical term. If a model does appear to have some use as the basis for a theory, then, apart from exploring its implications in detail, there is sometimes the possibility of experimenting on the model to see how it behaves. That is, if the model is not completely specified so that behaviour is the model is not deducible from its assumptions, then it is possible to conduct experiments to see how people behave in the circumstances in question. These experiments give information about behaviour only in the artificial situation but, if the judgement that the model will lead to a theory is correct, then there is the possibility that these experimental results will be capable of extension or interpretation into the more complex world described by the theory itself.

There are a variety of different sorts of tests available for a theory. We can discuss two forms. First, a theory as we have stated earlier, applies not just to a single event but to a class of events. There is therefore a natural division between, on the one hand, testing the class as a whole to see whether the group behaviour corresponds to that indicated by the theory, and on the other hand examining the individual elements within the class to see how far their behaviour corresponds to that suggested by the theory. For complex behaviour in a complex environment, it is unlikely that all of the elements in the class to which the theory applies will behave in exactly the way predicted. The propositions are statistical ones and single counter instances do not refute them. However, if there is sufficient knowledge about the individual items which deviate from the theory, one should be able to explain why each is a deviant by using a wider set of theoretical constructions.

The methods by which theories are tested in a group context are statistical. We look at the class as a whole, and without troubling about the individual deviants, observe whether or not this is consistent with what would be expected from the theory. Such processes are rather formalised, and for statistical operations there are 'significance tests' which broadly speaking give criteria for judging whether some supposed statistical regularity is genuine or could plausibly be a chance configuration.

Another form of observation is to look at the individual items and try to interpret their behaviour in terms of the available theory. Any deviance from the expected behaviour must be explicable in terms which do not mean that everything can be explained away in one sense or another. This is a 'case study' method. The case in question may have many attributes which can be described statistically so there is not a clear-cut division between case study and statistical methods. Statistics alone do not distinguish the two forms of activity from each other. The real characterisation comes in whether the testing is done on a group of the phenomena under discussion or on an individual element.

There are many different forms of case study ranging from seeking out the documents of some past event and analysing them in one way or another, to direct contact with the participants in some conflict. This last method is commonly done by meeting the parties to a conflict separately, if only because it is very difficult to get representatives to meet in cases where there is a great deal of tension. This obstacle has been overcome, not without considerable difficulty by Burton's 'controlled communication' method,[2] where, in one or two cases, the parties to a violent conflict have been persuaded to participate in a round-table meeting lasting for several sessions in the company of about an equal number of social scientists from various disciplines. This has proved fruitful for the parties themselves and also for the social scientists who were able to witness the changes in perceptions which went on as communication increased. The communication between conflicting parties cannot, of course, be observed if the parties are met with individually. In this sort of case-study context it is possible to examine theories of perception in conflict in a manner for which there is at the moment no other substitute.

This represents only a very stylised description of the relationship between theory and testing, and of some of the possible methods. It is not intended in any case as an exclusive categorisation. It is possible to represent in an equally stylised way the relationship of theory and testing through time. This is demonstrated in the diagram below.

We start in the box labelled 'unstructured observation'. This is the purely informal process of perceiving that there is a class of phenomena for which a theory is appropriate. It represents no formal step. A very simple model is then formulated which is not yet explanatory of the real world. This goes through the process of elaboration until it is at the level of testable theory. It is then tested and, if refuted, is either modified into a slightly different theory or rejected as hopeless. If modified, it goes the rounds again in the feed-back loop illustrated. If the theory passes the initial tests, it is then subjected to further tests which either put it back on the refutation path or send it round again on the testing cycle. Each time it survives the testing cycle, it acquires a greater degree of credence and the need to put it through further cycles diminishes. It never comes out of this cycle, however, as no theory is completely proved. The theory spends the rest of its days cycling around the retesting cycle unless at some point it is refuted and drops out to be modified. In point of fact, even theories of the highest standing seem to come out into the modification cycle from time to time in the light of some new evidence. In the case of theories in the social sciences, they are hardly anywhere else.

The problems which a social scientist tackles are different from those of the

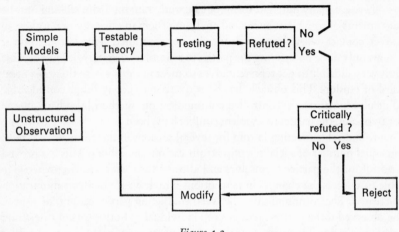

Figure 1.2

natural scientist, but nevertheless the general type of answer he is looking for is of the same form; that is, he is trying to make generalisations about classes of events, to talk of some events causing others and so on. There are, of course, many differences, though these are sometimes exaggerated.

Experiment is a very important technique in many of the natural sciences, whereas it plays only a minor role in the social sciences. This is sometimes regarded as meaning that, because of the very limited role of experiment, the social sciences cannot properly be regarded as sciences. This is, in effect, defining a scientific investigation as being an experimental investigation. This seems to be a misconception, however. Science is more conveniently defined in terms of the types of propositions it makes, namely generalisations about the behaviour of observable events. Experiment is only a technique, a very important technique, of course, in many areas, of suggesting and testing scientific hypotheses. It is perfectly possible to try out and test hypotheses in any other way which might prove convenient. The social scientist must observe his data in the raw, and cannot often design a little piece of the environment in order to test some hypothesis. However, to examine the world as it exists and analyse it by statistical and other methods, is in itself just as legitimate a method of procedure as to build artificial worlds in which to examine things.

Not all branches of natural science are privileged to use the experimental method, moreover. Both astronomers (in all their varieties) and meteorologists must take what nature gives them to observe, and have to use their ingenuity to wrest as much information as they can from what is given rather than to use it in devising new ways of influencing nature. The problem of the meteorologist has much in common with that of the economist. Both have a very complex system to analyse and both are tempted to give predictions. Physiologists are likewise restricted in the possibilities of experiment, though it is for social and ethical, rather than for natural, reasons that the possibilities of experiment on human beings are severely restricted.

Nor is experiment completely forbidden to the social scientist, though it is of course very restricted. The imposition of a 70 miles per hour speed limit on British roads was essentially an experiment. Psychologists carry out frequent experiments, though their difficulties in carrying over the results of experiments in severely restricted circumstances are more severe than the comparable problems for most natural scientists. The techniques of 'gaming' described in Chapter 9 are also experiments. Indeed, the role of experiment in the social sciences seems to be broadening the distinction between the experimental sciences and the non-experimental sciences is neither so clear cut nor so important as is sometimes alleged; nor does it correspond very closely with the distinction between the social and the natural sciences.

A second feature of the social sciences which it shares with the natural sciences, though to a more exaggerated degree, is the fact that in many situations the actual act of observation affects the phenomenon under survey. The observer, however little he wishes to, may become a participant in the situation. Thus if a social psychologist is trying to find out how a committee takes its decisions, then the knowledge that he is doing so may affect the members in ways not easily allowed for. If they know their decisions will be recorded, then they may, for example, act as they think they ought to act rather than as they would normally act without observation.

The prospect of observation, even at a future date, can influence either the decisions or the recording of decisions in wider contexts. Politicians like to appear in a favourable light, even to posterity. So, while the decisions themselves might be unaffected (which is far from certain), the recording of the decisions involved might be seriously distorted in the interests of providing a good public image. The observer has only the distorted records to go on. Some really crucial elements in many decision-making processes may go completely unrecorded as they are verbal, and any record the historian has consists of the very imperfect version based on what the decision makers and their advisers, when writing their memoirs, would like observers to think. The right of decision-makers to distort the recording of information by omission (a most powerful form of distortion) is clearly shown in the rule whereby observers are unable to see British Government documents until thirty years after the events with which they deal.

A variant of this problem is the question of the effect of statements made by observers on the subsequent course of events. The statement is itself a social act and may affect any decision taken, meaning that an event different from the one predicted occurs. For example, suppose a respected financial journalist predicts that some share will go up by 5%, all the readers of his column go out and buy the share. This puts up its price by 10%, thus falsifying the initial prophecy. Alternatively, if the share would have gone down but for the prediction, whereas in the event it goes up by 5%, the prediction has made the prophecy come true. The skilled observer can take account of the effects of the prediction itself and thus come up with the right answer. This, however, is not easy and is a complication from which natural scientists are mercifully preserved.

A further point is that an observer in the social sciences is a human being observing human beings. This is a two-edged weapon. In the first place, introspection can give an observer considerable insight into the possible actions of other human beings. It is a useful device for the preliminary selection of hypotheses. A social scientist can reason 'If I were a human being in that situation, I would do such and such.' This may not be what the subject of his research actually does, but at least it gives the observer an initial hypothesis to go on. The astronomer cannot say 'If I were a star in such and such a position, I would do that.' It would be nonsense. He has to rely entirely on the past observation of stars.

On the other hand, this approach has its dangers. Human beings differ, and one's own reactions to situations different from those one has experienced may be very different from what one images. It seems 'obvious' from introspection that the possibility of execution will deter people from murder. Statistical evidence does not bear out this 'obvious' proposition. When people achieve positions of great power, such as becoming the Prime Minister of Britain or the President of the U.S.A., they frequently begin to act in ways which appear inconsistent with their previous apparent attitudes. Unless one believes that they are complete hypocrites, one must assume that, once in their positions, they are subjected to pressures which it is hard to imagine without having experienced them. Introspection is a dangerous tool for finding out how people in such a position will act, as it will frequently give the wrong answer. The observer has to fall back on pure observation for the analysis of such situations. The difficulty is in sorting out those situations in which introspection is useful and those in which it is not. The observer, being human and exaggerating his own powers of understanding, probably uses it too much. The social sciences are full of faulty hypotheses which one suspects are largely derived from overconfidence in the reliability of introspection.

An issue which is commonly raised in connection with the social sciences, and which is often regarded, erroneously, as being their Achilles heel, is measurement. In physics, it is alleged, there are 'natural' schemes of measurement. In the social sciences there are not.

Now measurement is a form of classification. Thus, when we measure people according to age, we are fitting them into a particular class which distinguishes them from members of other classes. We can make these classifications of people as fine as we wish, or rather as fine as our measuring instruments will permit. What we commonly do with measurements is to relate an overall group arranged according to one characteristic, say age, with the same group divided by another characteristic, say height. Thus, we might say that, from birth to the age of sixteen, age and height increase with one another. By taking successive classes on the age classification, we find that they are also successively larger on the height classification, at least on average. This, in effect, is the purpose of this sort of measurement—to relate different classifications.

This example is relatively unambiguous. There is no problem about measuring either age or height. There are other issues, however, where it is not clear just what form of measure to use. A case in point is the measure of intelligence. We wish to classify people according to their intelligence in order to predict how they will act in other contexts. We set up a test and derive from this a measure of intelligence which comes out as an actual number, and is allegedly a characteristic of the individual in the same sense as his weight is. However, different tests and different conventions for deriving numbers from the tests might well yield different results. A measure's sole justification in the present context is its usefulness in prediction—not its 'naturalness'. In just the same way as we might argue of males aged thirty that, the heavier they are (classification 1), the more they will eat (classification 2), so we might argue of males aged thirty that, the higher they score in an intelligence test (classification 1), the quicker they learn Russian (classification 2). If psychologists can create this sort of measure, then it is perfectly legitimate to use it as a pragmatic device for making predictions. It stands and falls purely by its success in this role, and the question of whether it is a 'true' or a 'natural' measure does not really arise. It works.

This sort of problem arises constantly in the social sciences. Only infrequently are there measures which appear in any reasonable sense to be 'natural' or 'obvious'. In economics, money is often thought of as a naturally measurable variable, but closer investigation of many problems makes it clear that money values are only standing in for some other variable where the relationship is not always clear. However, as argued above, this does not matter too much. We are not asking of a measure that it is natural, but that it is workable. We can think of plausible measures for such things as hostility, cohesion, agreement and so on, but then we have to see it these measures are useful in prediction.

4 Peace and War: A Study for Social Scientists?

The study of war and peace is by no means new. A great deal of historical research has concerned itself with the study of particular wars in the past and libraries are filled with the resulting documentation and analysis. Military historians have discussed strategy and the methods of past wars. What might be called the political strategists such as Machiavelli and Clausewitz have discussed the uses of war as a tool of policy. Moralists such as St Thomas Aquinas have discussed the conditions under which, according to their moral code, war is justified. The study of the relations between states inevitably closely bound up with the study of war, has relatively recently been formalised under the title of International Relations. What, then, is there new in recent developments?

An academic discipline is characterised by two features. First, the questions it asks and, more problematically, those it answers. Secondly, the techniques which it uses to try to arrive at such answers. The broad questions which conflict theory asks are three—how and why do wars start, how and why do wars end, how do they proceed? These questions are, of course approached via a myriad of other questions, some of which in themselves may appear of smaller importance. The three questions are background questions rather than the titles of research topics; they also imply other questions. The answers to why wars start imply the answers to why wars do not start. From the point of view of the policy-maker, this may be the dominant interest.

Now, a historian interested in wars of the past can legitimately argue that he has been concerning himself with just these questions for a long time.

Theorists in international relations are also doing the same thing, and the boundary between the two groups is vague. Conflict Studies differs in the techniques it adopts. A historian is usually looking at particular events in the past and describing them in their own terms. A social scientist is looking for consistencies in behaviour in order to find theories of general classes of behaviour. Thus there is a substantial difference in the point of view of the historian and the social scientist. Superficially the questions appear to be the same, but behind the facade they are seen to be very different. The social scientist, by looking for theories of behaviour, expresses some implied belief that there are consistencies in behaviour, albeit of a complex nature. The historian is not required to deny such consistencies, but it is not his primary function to investigate them. In particular, he is not involved in attempting to define criteria for establishing the truth of various general propositions. 'Illuminating comparisons' is as far as his job takes him. The social scientist, however, is involved in establishing such criteria. There is not much point in establishing general propositions if he cannot say with what degree of confidence he holds them. A serious problem of inference faces the social scientist which the historian can avoid.

As far as the traditional study of international relations is concerned, the new approach merges into the old. To some extent, international relations has been the study, by the historical type of method, of relations between states as they are at the moment in relation to the immediate past. As such, it is more clearly associated with history in its methodology. However, there has grown up within the study of international relations a body of work which is more akin in style to the social science approach. The work of people like Karl Deutsch is characterised by a great interest in quantitative data and in the formulation of theories about the process of the behaviour of states which can be tested against data whether quantitative or not. This line has been pursued by a number of people who have come into the study from other fields, such as the natural and social sciences, and who see the formulation of testable hypotheses about behaviour as their job. There is a boundary between the approaches which is very ill defined. However, away from that boundary there is a very marked difference between the view of international relations as a branch of history verging on philosophy, and the view of it as a branch of the social sciences.

The issue is frequently raised that political events of the type we are considering are far too complicated to be dealt with in any scientific manner. The range of alternatives, it is argued, precludes any reasonable attempt to isolate critical elements from which to form a theory.

We should try to see just what is the substance of this argument. If something is said to be too complex for analysis, what is meant is that it is impracticable to analyse it, not that it is in principle impossible to analyse. However, argument from practicability can founder if new techniques are invented which make practicable the previously impracticable. A new tool which has arisen since the war and has vastly expanded our notions of what is practicable in the analysis of complicated situations is the computer.

The issue of complexity in itself is more serious if the ambition of an explanation is to explain everything. The fundamentals of a situation are often simple. A basic theory will often explain most of what happens, though the extension of the theory to explain the residual details might be beyond the bounds of practicability. It is conceivable that the search for basic theories of political events which will explain the bulk of situations will be fruitless. There seems no particular reason to be so pessimistic, though, particularly when we recognise that the degree of complexity we can handle is considerable.

5 The Level of Analysis

In the discussion of any problem, it must be decided in what particular framework the analysis should be conducted, and at what level of generality the questions should be posed. Conflict is no exception to this. A whole range of questions can be asked, and it appears that many misunderstandings of the purposes of the study of conflict arise simply because the answers produced are assumed to be answers to another set of questions, for which the answers given are clearly inappropriate or irrelevant.

Divisions of the level of analysis are, of course, arbitrary, but it is convenient to adopt the following scheme which we shall illustrate after describing it. The first level is that of the individual actor or event, in which the analysis is in terms of the peculiarities of the individual. It stresses the uniqueness of the individual event. The second level of analysis is to recognise the particular events as individual, but endeavour to relate them to broader categories of similar events. Though the event is still seen as unique, the stress is on its connections with other like events. The interest is in the individual event, but the knowledge gained about it is found by comparison with other members of the class of which it is a member. The final level is the most general of all, in which we seek to understand the general behaviour of classes of events and are uninterested in the idiosyncrasies of the particular individual units. The first two of these levels concern the behaviour of individuals, though from rather different perspectives; the third is concerned with the study of a different sort of phenomenon, namely the group of events, as opposed to the individual components.

This can be illustrated by reference to the various analyses which can be done of suicide—a phenomenon which is of interest to behavioural and social scientists. Every suicide is a unique event, and the result of a whole set of complex interactions of pressures and influences on an individual who has his own unique personality formed from his lifetime experiences. A particular suicide can be described in terms of the individual alone, and as an event peculiar to this individual. If one were to examine an individual suicide in a very personal sense, then one would despair of formulating a theory of suicide. It would all appear too particular and special. The understanding of suicide would seem to be more the concern of literature than of science.

However, a psychiatrist might view the problem somewhat differently (and for his purposes we must assume that the suicide had either failed, or was still in the ranks of the suicide-prone). The problem would still be one of examining an individual, but the basis of the examination would be what the patient shared with others and not in what ways he differed. The psychiatrist has a body of theory which states that, when individuals are placed in various types of situation, they develop certain characteristics. He can divide people into various classes—manic depressive, paranoid and so on— such that he can classify their reactions to various situations, and suggest what sort of therapy would bring about an improvement in the patient's condition. He is using his knowledge of the behaviour of classes of events in order to classify his patient and relate the individual to his theories in order to explain his behaviour in its terms. He is not denying that the patient is an individual and that his condition will deviate from the 'pure' case of whatever he is suffering from. Indeed, the patient may have his own peculiar combination of symptoms which the psychiatrist has never seen before in quite that form. However, he can realistically talk of explaining the behaviour of the individual in terms of propositions derived from the observation of large classes of individuals.

Clearly, these two classes are likely to overlap with each other. However much an event is described as unique, it is nevertheless placed in a context of other events, and indeed it is only by relating it to other events that it can be referred to as unique. The two classes represent the different ends of a spectrum rather than clearly demarcated classifications.

The third form of analysis of suicide is represented by the sociologist's approach. Here it is the behaviour of groups of individuals which is the predominant concern. We are more interested in explaining, say, why the suicide rate in Norway is very much lower than that in either Sweden or

Denmark, despite the obvious similarities between the societies. In this case we are not trying to explain each particular suicide. Each suicide in each country is a unique event explicable in terms of a unique set of personal circumstances. However, it is hard to believe that the differences in suicide rates between the two countries are completely accidental, and, in default of finding any differences in the statistical definition of suicide, we have to assume that there are factors absent (or present) in Norway which make these individual events less likely there. The propositions made by the examiner of this problem will be propositions about groups, and deviant individuals will readily be found in all the countries concerned, but this is not of importance.

Again, the classification of the problems is not absolute, and there is a clear overlap between an analysis on the group level and the analysis on the individual level. The propositions made by the psychiatrist about the individual owe their origin to propositions about groups, while the propositions about the group are likewise not divorced from propositions about the individual. There is an overlap, but nevertheless there are distinct problems.

A similar sort of categorisation exists in economics, where a problem can be analysed at various different levels. The most individual level is that which deals with the history of one particular firm. Firm histories (of which there are many) talk of the particular events that impinged upon the firm which made it successful (the histories of unsuccessful firms are less frequently written). Various factors such as the personalities of the owners and general leaders of the firm will be discussed, and the influence of these personalities on the behaviour of the firm will be analysed. Indeed, it is possible to read firm histories and decide that business behaviour can be explained only in terms of the personalities of the people involved, in much the same way as it is frequently alleged that the behaviour of states is explicable only in terms of the personalities of their leaders. However, this is not always satisfactory to an economist. He frequently wants to explain the behaviour of a firm or market in more general terms, that is, in terms of a general theory of a firm's behaviour. Thus he endeavours to explain why a firm or group of firms starts to increase or decrease its price at a particular time and, in order to do this, he begins to utilise general propositions concerning price formation such as are embodied, for example, in the well-known laws of supply and demand. In this sort of question he is utilising more general propositions about classes of events to explain a particular event.

Finally, the economist might be interested in the general problem of why firms behave in particular ways, such as why they expand, and here the emphasis is not on the behaviour of a particular firm, which may be a deviant, but on the behaviour of firms as a whole. Thus, an expansion in the building industry might be explained in terms of higher prices of houses, making for bigger profits in building. It neglects the odd firm which went into bankruptcy because its owner was a dipsomaniac. However, this general proposition still relates to propositions about individuals in that, to arrive at it, there is a process of setting up some 'representative firm' whose behaviour can be treated as being typical of the group. Thus, this category of analysis is not rigorously demarcated from the earlier category of individual firms.

These levels of analysis are not mutually exclusive, and an analysis at one level does not preclude an analysis at another, which is equally valid. It all depends on the type of study and the type of questions which need to be asked. The problems posed at the 'history of the firm' level are different from those asked when the behaviour of the industrial system as a whole is at issue. For details of behaviour, an analysis of personalities is required, but for other types of questions it is almost irrelevant; so it is important to be clear just what sort of level of analysis one is actually involved in.

The level of analysis problem similarly appears in the study of international relations. Traditionally, international relations has been studied from a historical point of view, which is really an examination of questions at the first level of analysis—that is an examination of essentially unique events, whose detailed behaviour we seek to understand. It is inevitable that such a study stresses the unique aspects of the problems, and explanations of events in terms of the personalities of the actors are common. However, other levels of analysis are appropriate too, and one can almost describe conflict studies (or at least those parts of conflict studies which deal with international relations) as the posing of questions at the two more general levels of analysis. This is something of a distortion, as historians, as much as anyone else, describe their unique events in terms of implicit theories of behaviour. Nevertheless, it is not unfair to suggest that the historian is professionally more prone to consider the unique aspects of behaviour, whereas the social scientist tends to emphasise the similarities.

6 The Origins of Conflict Studies

It is only comparatively recently that the causes of peace and war have been regarded as suitable material for classification, generalisation, and detailed theorisation. Grand theories of war have appeared as features of grand theories of society, but the analysis of war has taken the form of detailed analysis of particular wars, rather than the analysis of war as an aspect of human behaviour in a way analogous to that in which economic behaviour is analysed.

One relatively early attempt at a genuine scientific theory of war was that propounded by Hobson[3] and subsequently adapted by Lenin[4]. This theory asserted that war is the result of clashes in a colonial struggle. The capitalists of one nation find that the rate of return on their capital in domestic investment falls. More profitable lines of investment are to be found in what are now referred to as underdeveloped countries. However, the capitalists of other states are similarly involved in exploiting the poorer areas the world. So long as there are plenty of areas to be exploited, capitalists can keep out of each other's way, but as the supply of virgin territory is lapped up they come into conflict. As, according to the Marxist theory, the state is the tool of the ruling classes, in this case the capitalists, the various groups can call upon the assistance of their states to help enforce their own particular claims. The states thus come into conflict and war ensues.

As a theory of war, this seemed a much more plausible description of the activities of both major (and minor) European powers in the early part of the twentieth century, when it was propounded, than it does today. However, whatever its merits as a description of a particular class of wars, it is clearly severely lacking as a general theory of war. There are too many counter-examples, where this explanation of the readiness to fight wars is clearly inadequate. We must give this explanation of war credit for being an attempt to formulate a general theory, however convenient it happened to be ideologically, but fault it for its inadequacy. Unfortunately, in honesty one has to admit that there still exists nothing even resembling an adequate theory to fill the vacuum.

The development of the study of war as a branch of the social sciences began much more clearly after the first world war, as one of the results of this traumatic experience of Western societies. The surprise is not perhaps that the war, which completely shattered the earlier view, held particularly in Britain, that man had at last achieved a safe and developing society, stimulated such work, but that it did not stimulate more. Lewis Fry Richardson, an English Quaker, struggled alone to produce a remarkable mathematical and statistical discussion of the problems of war; and Quincy Wright, the leader of a group working at the University of Chicago, produced in 1947 an enormous book called *A Study of War*[5] in which he tried to encompass all approaches to war which had been made.

It is without disrespect to the other pioneers of a more scientific approach to the study of conflict that we attribute to Richardson the pre-eminent position amongst the scholars who originated work in this field. His conceptions were bold, and their marks are visible on a great deal of the work which is described in this book. He was the first person in this field to recognise that, not only is it necessary to collect statistical data, but also to test hypotheses by statistical means. A similar development was going on in economics at the same time, but Richardson was unaware of this. It was accepted in economics (though not always without reluctance), but, in the study of international behaviour, it was regarded as most strange. It is not until recently that such an approach has been regarded as a legitimate form of intellectual activity—and even today it is rejected by many.

Richardson was, in fact, not a social scientist, but a meteorologist. He did his work on the causes of war in the period from the end of the first world war until his death in 1950. His major contributions are contained in two books published posthumously, *Arms and Insecurity*[6] and *Statistics of Deadly Quarrels*[7]. It is an interesting comment on the rapid changes in attitude towards this approach that, while Richardson is now accorded great respect even by those who disagree with this type of work, his editors (all of whom were eminent men in their own fields—one, in fact, was Quincy Wright) had considerable difficulty finding a publisher to take on the books.

Richardson's early training was in physics, from which he moved into meteorology. His reputation as an innovator in that field is very high and, on the strength of it, he was elected a Fellow of the Royal Society. In 1922 he published a classic work on meteorology called *Weather Prediction by Numerical Process*[8]. With the facilities available at the time, the procedures he suggested were impracticable, as, by the time any prediction had been made, the weather supposedly predicted would have long since passed. However, the modern electronic computer has largely overcome this aspect of the problem, and his work lies at the basis of much current prediction method.

Since the second world war there has been a much heightened interest in the study of the cause of war, and social scientists have entered the field in a serious manner. The causes of this development seem to be two. First, trauma upon trauma has hit the world in the twentieth century. Not merely did the second world war show that the claim that the first one was 'a war to end wars' was nothing but a naïve and pious hope, but, even before the second war had ended, the third one appeared to be in view. The invention of the atomic bomb, and subsequently the hydrogen bomb, made the slogan 'The end of the world is at hand' more than the warning of a pathetic evangelist. A war between the Soviet Union and the United States could, and probably would, obliterate society as we know it.

In such circumstances, it is not surprising that scholars who feel their discipline might have something to offer (and those range from zoologists to statisticians to psychoanalysts) should attempt to make what applications they can.

The second reason for the burst of interest by social scientists in the problem of war and peace is the remarkable development of their techniques since the end of the second world war. The statistical testing of hypotheses in such subjects as economics, still in its infancy before the war, has progressed enormously. Further, the invention of the computer and its now quite widespread accessibility, has immensely extended the scope of the social scientist's analysis. Both as a tool for the processing of large amounts of information and for complicated simulation, the computer is of vast importance and may well be on the way to revolutionising the whole of the social sciences. It has been described by one pair of writers as comparable in importance for both natural and social scientists to the microscope and telescope for natural scientists[9].

Thus we have two reasons for the development of the social science approach since the second world war: the fact that a crucial problem exists to be solved makes it natural for the social scientist to attempt to do something about it; and the reinforcement of this desire by the fact that he is now in a position actually to do something—which until recently, he was not.

chapter two

Aggression and War

1 The Relevance of Aggression

A basic problem in the study of violence is whether there is a basic problem. In a sense, mankind possesses basic aggressive drives which, like sexual instincts, motivate him in unconscious ways and barely conscious. How relevant this is to the study of the causes of war is not clear. In one sense it is a problem so fundamental that it ceases to be of interest for the scholar who is interested in more mundane questions. Its partial relevance, and the claims made for it to be of even greater relevance, are considered in this chapter.

To say that mankind has a basic aggressive drive is not the same as saying that man is innately and irremediably violent—which is, perhaps, as well. It is undoubtedly the case that some individuals endeavour to become leaders in their groups or, more generally, that human beings endeavour to dominate their environment, including those parts of their environment consisting of other people. If there are several aggressive people in the group, then a conflict is generated which may be resolved by one person winning or may result in a more or less permanent battle. Conflict is clearly not universally abhorred and indeed there seem to be many people who are quite clearly unhappy without it. What is less clear is how this sense of aggression is converted into lethal fighting, which is another frequent occupation of mankind. Presumably there is some connection, but what it is is obscure.

We should be careful to distinguish between two ways in which the word 'aggression' is used in connection with war. Both usages are, in any case, rather loose. First, a country is called aggressive if it initiates warfare without 'due cause' (a usefully flexible term which enables everyone to be in the right). Secondly, we talk of human beings being aggressive in the sense that they enjoy warfare, are willing, perhaps subconsciously, to provoke it for its own sake and, in its absence, require some strenuous physical, emotional or intellectual effort by way of sublimation. This sort of aggression we shall refer to as biological aggression in cases where there is ambiguity.

Now it is not self-evident that biological aggression necessarily leads to war or even that war can be predominantly explained in its terms. At some stage, of course, a necessary condition for warfare to exist as an institution is that people are prepared to fight, and this could be regarded as an exemplification of the aggressive instinct.

However, suppose it were to prove possible to re-direct to some extent the aggressive drives of human beings. Would this have a great deal of effect on the frequency and intensity of war? This is doubtful, but still an open question. Different countries with rather similar social systems (Britain and Sweden, for example) have radically different patterns of behaviour regarding their participation in wars, and these are hard to explain solely or even partly in terms of inherent differences in aggressive make-up.

This is not to argue that there is no point in looking at the problem of biological aggression even if suggestions for policy are unlikely to emerge from such a study. At some level, war is made possible by people's willingness to fight, and an understanding of the background issues involved in a problem is very useful for grasping the more practical points. At some stage, this understanding might even have implications for the design of our societies. However, even a good analysis of the fundamental problem of aggression would only be of limited help in adjusting human societies so that they avoid war. The more down to earth issues are of greater practical significance for this purpose.

2 The Uses and Abuses of Aggression

One need not be a committed Freudian, or indeed the follower of any other school of analytical psychology, to accept that the instinctual drives which served a useful purpose in preserving and developing the human species in a primitive form of society, are still there. However, these require serious modification in form for the effective development of highly complex modern human societies. That such drives come out, and serve some clearly disfunctional purpose in modern society, is not too surprising.

The study of conflict from this fundamental point of view has proceeded along two tracks. Biologists have studied animal conflict, partly as a means of analogy, and partly because some knowledge of the animal elements in human behaviour might yield insights which would enable it to be more reliably controlled. The other strand of thought is that of the analytical psychologists (notably the Freudian psycho-analysts) who proceed on the not dissimilar lines of pointing out that the so-called rational processes of decision are heavily determined by subconscious motives which can be very disfunctional in complex societies.

Man is a mammal and has much in common with other mammals, and indeed with all other sorts of animals[10]. Physiologically, there is a great deal that can be learned about the human body from the examination of animals and, perhaps to a more limited extent, there are things to be learned about psychological behaviour from animal conduct. Certainly a large number of psychologist man-hours have been devoted to the psychology of the rat in the hope of finding out about such branches of knowledge as the learning processes of men (and rats); so it is not outrageous to suggest that some clues to man's social behaviour might be gleaned from the social behaviour of animals.

This sort of study, however, should be approached with extreme caution. Mankind in human society is very different from animals in animal society. Man differs from the animals in being highly intelligent and, partly as a consequence of this, he has developed extremely sophisticated languages in order to communicate very complex and subtle ideas to other members of his species. As far as we know, no animal has a means of communication as effective as language in the sense in which it is understood by humans. Because of his high intelligence and elaborate language, it has been possible for man to develop societies of extreme complexity. The overriding difference between human society and animal society is that man can, in some rather vague way, design the society he wishes to live in. Even if 'design' appears too strong a word, human society certainly alters at what, by evolutionary standards, is a phenomenal rate. Human society today is radically different from that of a thousand years ago, whereas colonies of rats or herds of gorillas behave in much the same way as they did then. Animals alter their social behaviour only when the environment changes in such a manner as to force adaptation. Humans can alter their social structure autonomously and without the impetus of environmental change.

The differences, then, between animal and human society are striking, and one should be very cautious in assuming that, because some animal society reacts in certain ways to certain events, it follows that human societies will react in a similar way. Humans have a very much wider choice of methods of adaptation. In spite of these differences, the study of animals raises certain questions which are worth examining, even though we might be legitimately cautious in applying the answers to human beings. For example, it has been shown that animals which are quite amiable to members of their own species when they are out in their natural habitat become quite ferocious and fight to the death in the more cramped quarters of the zoo. This raises the interesting question of whether all animals, including humans, get more aggressive when put in cramped quarters. However, once the question is raised—but for this study it is quite possible that it would not have been—the answer must be looked for in entirely human terms: it does not follow that we shall all imitate the monkeys in becoming more and more destructive as we move into bigger cities. Indeed, any evidence that we do seems far from strong. The question, though, is interesting and should be pursued, acknowledging the fact that it was in the context of animal behaviour it was suggested.

If we look at animal societies, aggressive instincts do have some clear purpose, particularly as fighting rarely involves the death of the losers. In the case of foraging animals, the more evenly spaced they are over some territory in which there is food, the better they will be able to do for themselves as a group. So, if animals attack each other when they trespass on each other's territory, this even spreading-about is achieved. The fighting here serves a useful purpose. Similarly, a species is likely to be best preserved if its physically stronger members breed the most, as they are most likely to produce strong offspring. One way of deciding physical strength is to fight, as stags do, and the winner (who is normally the stronger) mates with the doe, with the greater likelihood of producing healthy, strong offspring. This is good from a species preservation point of view, particularly as the losing stag is not killed, and might therefore get some less desirable doe. Presumably the ones who lose out are the weak stags who are unable to beat anyone. This is sad for them, but not for the species.

It would be hard for an observer from Mars to see precisely what species preservation function was served by human warfare. There have, of course, been suggestions that war weeded out the weak from the strong and that this, in some sense, purifies the race. These views now seem obscene and inappropriate to modern society. However, this is not to say that aggression diverted into appropriate channels is not vital to the creation of a modern society. It might be that creative activity of any kind, artistic or scientific, comes from the channelling of aggressive instincts in appropriate directions. It is, however, necessary that this channelling occur. When it goes into violent conflict it seems to serve no useful function to the human species.

There are, of course, many other drives which do not serve their original animal functions or, if they do, do so only in a very limited form. Freud was much criticised for overemphasising the repression of the sexual drive required in modern society as the predominant factor in psychological illness. He modified his views in his later work, but continued to give great emphasis to the subjugation of the sexual drive [11, 12], and few would deny that it is of great importance. The sexual drive and sexual activity very rarely serve their basic, biological purpose, procreation. The overwhelming majority of acts of sexual intercourse performed by human beings are done for love or pleasure. Only occasionally is the prime motive the production of babies.

Fortunately, this has no disfunctional effects on human society—in fact the reverse—in marked contrast with the urges to violence.

At an earlier stage of the development of human society, the aggressive instincts of man served a purpose clearly analogous to that which the same sort of instincts serve in other primates. The establishment of leadership patterns, the need to develop good hunters, and the usefulness of keeping different tribes of people apart to spread out the supply of potential food all combined to make the aggressive attribute a useful one. However, while there still exist needs to establish such things as leadership patterns, it is less obvious that a capacity for physical violence is the best way of doing this.

By and large violence is not a device used within domestic societies for adjudicating their leadership problems. However, the impulse to violence remains, and it is conceivable that their partially suppressed manifestations are at the root of the readiness of people, when organised into nations, to seek recourse to violent conflict to solve their disagreements.

It is still sometimes argued that warfare does bring some benefits to society, and is thus not completely disfunctional. These arguments take on a variety of forms. It is possible to find those who hold a mystical view of the moral virtues of war, and of the nobility of death in action. If these virtues were not to have an opportunity to display themselves, it is argued, mankind would be poorer and would become effete. Such opinions are now rather démodé. Others suggest that warfare is at least useful in that it speeds up technical progress with benefits to the world at large. It is possible that aircraft would be less advanced today but for the impact of the demand for high-performance military aircraft. The issue here is whether it is worth it.

Clearly, whether one regards warfare as having a use or not depends on the moral judgements one is prepared to make. Few codes of ethics would give warfare absolutely no redeeming feature. The issue seems to be whether the redeeming features are worth the enormous costs.

3 Aggression as a Concept in Political Analysis

In the last few decades, whenever one country has gone to war with another, it has been customary for both to claim that the other was the aggressor. This is the political use of the word aggression discussed in the first section. The term is in such disrepute through its extensive propaganda use that claims of aggression are not taken seriously, except by the more partisan supporters of one or the other side in such disputes. The notion that warfare is essentially initiated by an aggressor against a victim has been firmly entrenched in the thinking behind both the League of Nations and the United Nations, with stern disapprobation shown towards countries acting aggressively. This is unfortunate. Why countries go to war at all is obscure, once one moves out of the world of the politician. To present war in terms of a naïvely simple conflict between virtue and sin, as in a second-rate cowboy film, hinders the analysis of the problem and obscures its results. This approach is akin to regarding the breakdown of marriage as being due to a matrimonial offence. The belief that war is caused by an aggressor and divorce by a sinner both involve similar and equally fruitless attitudes. It is much more useful to conceive of both problems as involving the breakdown of a system, an analysis which avails itself less freely of moral judgements.

This is not to deny that some nations have a more permissive attitude to violence, and are willing to consider war as an instrument of policy much more readily than are others. This is a phenomenon which wants explaining rather than condemning. It is clearly a very different question from that of attempting to determine the aggressor in a war in some narrow legal sense, the difficulties of which are, in any case, well known.

The political concept of aggression has limited use in the dispassionate analysis of the warlike relationships between states. One use which is free from the drawbacks discussed is that made by Johan Galtung[13]. He proposes a theory whereby aggressive behaviour, defined as 'drives towards change, even against the will of others', comes about when there is 'rank disequilibrium'. This term is best explained by defining its converse, 'rank equilibrium'. An individual in society has status in a number of dimensions such as income, education, social respectability and so on. He is said to be in rank equilibrium if he is either high or low in all of these dimensions, so that there is no conflict in status. He is in 'rank disequilibrium' if he is high on some and low on others. Hence, a person who is wealthy but poorly educated is in rank disequilibrium, and aggressive behaviour, it is hypothesised, is associated with this condition. The theory can be interpreted in terms of social groups as well as individual people, and it is thereby conceivable that nations are more aggressive when in rank disequilibrium. It is not quite clear whether this theory is true or false or what are the appropriate dimensions, but it is an illuminating way of posing the problem and is an attempt to understand rather than to condemn aggression.

Biological concepts of aggression may also illuminate the political problem of the violence which takes place within nations, and the growth of creeds and doctrines which glorify the violent and warlike state. Thus we can describe as aggressive behaviour the attacks on minority racial or religious groups, and indeed, attacks on supposedly harmful individuals such as witches. The most notorious of these doctrines, of course, is that which led to the violent attacks on Jews in Nazi Germany, but there has been a persistent history of violence against the Jews in most countries. The Negroes in the Southern States of the United States are the targets of intermittent violence and, in the past, were much more so. Much interracial violence is more or less independent of the international scene. However, in the case of Hitler's Germany there was a clear relationship: Nazism was a creed which was specifically dedicated to the glorification of violence and the belief in an expansionary national state which was perfectly entitled to get its ends by war. This view had popular backing in Germany during the 1930s.

We are not, of course, completely without any explanation of the rise of Nazism. Humiliation in war coupled with extreme forms of poverty due to damage in war, the enormous reparations which were demanded by other countries, and severe economic depression would not unnaturally incline people away from the more polite and restrained forms of political expression. However, the mechanism of the move from social frustration to social explosion needs more examination, along with realistic appraisals of how to contain such violence. In this area it would seem that a knowledge and understanding of the problem of biological aggression could have considerable significance.

The study of biological aggression also has some relevance in the case of international conflict, partly for the same reasons as for domestic conflict. In any case, the borderlines between international and internal conflict are rather tenuous and artificial in such cases as Algeria or Vietnam. While it seems doubtful that these studies can yield any immediately useful results, this is not really a criticism. Many who are doing research into the problem of conflict are clearly bent on the improvement of the world—the intellectual do-gooders—but, even if their findings turn out to be unusable for political or other reasons, there is still the virtue of knowledge for its own sake. In any case, for the functionally inclined, this research may find its uses at some stage.

Clearly, the basic value of a study of biological aggression, if and when it materialises, is in showing where the constraints on any attempt to design any social structure lie. The drives behind human conduct such as the aggressive and the sexual drives, are very strong and deep-rooted, and attempts to stop them, except under very special circumstances, are likely either to fail or to produce some very undesirable side-effects. Control must be seen as a process of steering rather than a process of stopping, though how the subconscious proclivities to violence are to be contained in a complex society is still regrettably obscure.

chapter three

The Statistical Description of War

1 War as a Suitable Subject for Statistical Analysis

Statistics is a method of analysing groups of phenomena. Thus, for example, we might take a group of events such as the number of live births which take place in the United Kingdom in some particular year. If we are interested in infant mortality, then we may also count the number of the children born in the year who die within a year of their birth. For convenience, we will probably present the number of babies who die as a percentage of the total births, and call this the infant mortality rate. However, it is likely that our basic purpose in collecting such statistics is to find out the causes of infant mortality with a view to reducing it. Thus we might split births up into those which take place in hospital and those which take place elsewhere to see if the infant mortality rate is the same in each group. If it is different, then we explore, by various standard techniques, whether it is likely that the discrepancy in the infant mortality rates could reasonably be ascribed to chance, or whether there may be some reason for there being a difference. If we discover it is unlikely to be chance, then we can further refine the questions and ask whether it makes any difference whether the baby is delivered by a doctor or a midwife. We can go on in this way, grouping the births of babies in various different ways, to see what factors relate consistently to high and low infant mortality. In other words, we are using an analysis of the group of events in order to see if we can pick out factors which are causes of infant mortality in a situation in which we suppose that there are many causes.

Now, this sort of approach is extremely useful when we are considering very large groups of events such as the birth of children. When we are dealing with small groups of events, the method is much less reliable. Suppose we are interested in the relationship between the birth weight of a child and the weight of the mother. If we examine a thousand instances, we will find a fairly close relationship. However, there will be a number of individual deviations. If we examine only ten cases, we may not find much relationship, as it is quite possible that a group of only ten will consist entirely of deviants. Our observations may still be interesting, but we must treat any conclusions with caution.

Wars are events which take place with great frequency in social life. We discuss just how frequently in section 3. We might then tentatively assume that statistical analysis might give us some insights into the causes of war, by the rather indirect method of suggesting factors which are related to each other. Simply getting a relationship is not, of course, by itself telling us that there is a causal relationship present, but it does give us some idea of where to start our theorising.

The objection to using a statistical analysis of war, which is made by classical historical theorists of the international system, is that all wars are different. This, however, is true of other social events to which statistical analysis is applied: suicides are all different. To understand why a given person attempted suicide, one must delve very deeply into his character and whole experience, but the uniqueness of each individual suicide does not preclude us from making some very interesting comments about suicide derived from statistical study, such as that suicide is much more frequent amongst people with no fixed home than amongst the population as a whole. This does not necessarily mean that transience breeds suicide—we must look more deeply and see why people are transient—but it does give us some information about suicides, which will not apply to every single case, but which is of use in trying to discover the reasons for people committing suicide. The same is true of war. All wars are different, but it seems unlikely that, of the 315 wars reported by Richardson [7] as having taken place between 1820 and 1949, some characteristics were not shared by groups of wars. It seems more plausible to hypothesise that there are some connecting links than that there are none. In view of the frequency of war, it is certainly worth a try.

The wars that we fight or threaten to fight today are not, of course, the same as those we fought a century ago. The speed of communications and the vast change in arms (improvement seems hardly the word) combine to make war different in many significant respects. War, however, has still not altered completely. The world is still divided into nation states and many of today's states—particularly those which do a lot of the fighting and the threatening—were in existence in some form or another a hundred years ago. The human beings involved in making the decisions, still largely and then exclusively men, are much the same as they were. They still take decisions in similar small groups such as cabinets and, while these groups may in many cases be more responsive to public opinion than they were, they can contrive to manage a great deal of independence, particularly in cases of war. Indeed, even in societies as open and libertarian as Britain, the decision takers succeed in keeping a great deal of the really crucial information secret at the time the decisions are made. The Suez Crisis of 1956 illustrated this quite clearly. Thus, nuclear bombs, supersonic fighters and literate generals notwithstanding, there are some common elements in the present-day decision processes that pertain to war, which are similar to those of earlier times. While it might be foolish to assume that we can simply generalise from the past to the present, it would be equally foolish to assume that there is nothing to be learned from the past. To know what caused past wars may well give us some insight into what causes present and will cause future ones.

The statistical approach is essentially that of standing as far back as possible from the phenomenon under study to see what can be learned by so doing. It is the extreme case of looking for the pattern unencumbered by the individual case. One can examine social phenomena from different ranges in order to get different perspectives on the various problems in hand. One can, for instance, move in very close and examine the behaviour of a single decision maker in a single crisis—there have already been studies of the late President Kennedy during his brief but eventful Presidency of the United States [14, 15]. This sort of approach is at the other end of the spectrum from the statistical. It gives its own insights and forms of understanding which would be undetected by a more sweeping approach. On the other hand, such concern for the particular inevitably obscures the relationship of events to the broader class of events to which they belong. As we have earlier emphasised, the social sciences are primarily concerned with the consistencies between events and their classification into groups. The grouping according to numerical attributes is an extreme case of this.

2 The Size of Wars

A study of war, or for that matter of any other phenomenon, involves the classifying of the data in some manner. Obvious ways of classifying wars are according to who fights in them, the number of participants, the type of cause, and so on. One important basis for classification is the size of the war. This is an obvious way of getting some indication of its importance and, in any case, the size itself is a matter of significance. In this section we shall discuss the way in which Richardson and most subsequent writers approached this problem of size, and the difficulties involved in discussing it.

One indicator of the size of a war which suggests itself immediately is the number of people killed. Other possibilities are the amount of destruction or the number of people both killed and injured. The objection to the first of these other possibilities is that it is very difficult to measure, both because of the difficulty of getting the raw data and then of valuing it. Monetary value is, at best, a crude guide, and the fact that there are a number of doubtful stages which intervene in trying to compare the value of a peasant's hut destroyed in 1870 with a power station destroyed in 1940 is obvious. However, a death occurring in 1870 and one in 1940 are much more obviously comparable, even though the first may have taken place in a trench and the second in a submarine. The difficulty with the other measure lies in the definition of wounded, which can vary widely. Furthermore, counts of wounded, particularily in earlier wars, were very rough and ready. The figures of people dead are much more likely to have some semblance of accuracy—not much, as the very different estimates of deaths for the same battles testify—or at least to be more dependable than those based on any other criterion.

A virtue of using size as a classification system is that it is reasonably objective and does not run into any difficulties concerning the legal definition of war. For the purposes of the social scientist (and at the other extreme, of the moralist), all we are interested in is that a large-scale, violent conflict involving deaths took place. Many large conflicts were not international wars. In recent times, neither the Spanish Civil War nor the Algerian War were officially classified as wars between powers. To exclude them from the analysis of violence would, however, be foolish. The distinctions between, say, revolutions, civil wars and international wars may, of course, be important, even from the point of view of the social scientist, but ignoring these distinctions may also be revealing, and the size criterion effectively does this.

Size classification, in getting round one difficulty of definition leads itself in another one. When is a violent conflict too small to be called war? Richardson tackles this problem very bluntly by making no distinction between world war, on the one hand, and murders on the other. All are instances of 'deadly quarrels'. This might seem too extreme in the sense that the factors affecting the murder rate are not likely to be the same as those causing war. A theory covering both sets of phenomena is likely to be too general to say very much. The question, however, need not trouble us here, as none of the propositions about wars depend on the number of murders.

Superficially, the most obvious way of listing wars according to the number of deaths would be to have columns headed 0 to 10,000, 10,000 to 20,000 and so on. This procedure has a number of disadvantages, however. In dealing with numbers which vary very widely in magnitude, we most naturally think in terms of one war involving ten times as many deaths as another, or half as many or whatever the case may be. Thus we would normally feel that a war with 1,500 deaths was a rather different affair from one involving 9,500 deaths, and should be categorised separately. However, two wars involving respectively 101,500 and 109,500 deaths appear much the same from a size point of view. Accordingly, it is easier to comprehend if we divide our categories to reflect this, that is, in a proportional manner rather than according to the direct numbers involved.

Richardson suggested categories of this proportional type. The basis of his categorisation was that the biggest war which could be fitted into one category should be one-tenth of the size of the biggest war which may be fitted into the next category. Thus, we get the following list:

Category	Size	Range
A	1 to 10	$= 10^0$ to 10^1
B	10 to 100	$= 10^1$ to 10^2
C	100 to 1,000	$= 10^2$ to 10^3
D	1,000 to 10,000	$= 10^3$ to 10^4
E	10,000 to 100,000	$= 10^4$ to 10^5
F	100,000 to 1,000,000	$= 10^5$ to 10^6
G	1,000,000 to 10,000,000	$= 10^6$ to 10^7

As readers familiar with the concept of logarithms* will know, we can represent any number as ten to some power or other. Thus 50,000 can be approximately represented as $10^{4.7}$. The logarithm of the number of deaths gives us a convenient measure of the size of a war. Following Richardson, we shall define the logarithm (to base 10) of the number of deaths as the *magnitude* of the war. Thus a war of magnitude 6 is a war in which 1,000,000 people died.

Richardson, did not, in fact, use exactly these classes and, instead of using say 10^4 as the end point of one class and the beginning of another, he shifted the classes so that the logarithm of this was the middle point. In the table opposite we give, alongside the magnitudes, the numbers of deaths in ordinary numbers which these represent, and the number of wars in each category which occurred.

There is a big virtue in representing the size of wars in this way which is connected with our earlier point about proportional sizes being in some sense the most significant measure. The estimates of war deaths are very inaccurate. With

* Readers unfamiliar with logarithms (or who have forgotten about them) need not worry providing they will take a little on trust. A number such as a thousand can be written as $10 \times 10 \times 10$ or more concisely as 10^3. This is referred to as '10 raised to the power 3' 3 is called the *logarithm* of 1,000. Numbers which are not exact powers of ten like 100 and 1,000 still can be represented in this way. Corresponding to any number between say 100 and 1,000 there is a power between 2 and 3 to which 10 can be raised corresponding to that number. Thus 357 can be written as $10^{2.55267}$.

the best will in the world, they are likely to involve considerable amounts of guesswork. This best will is rarely, in fact, to be found. Participants in war have both conscious and unconscious motives for misrepresenting the number dead—usually (though not always) with a view to under-estimating their own dead and exaggerating the enemy's. This leads to a range of estimates in which the highest might be two or three times the lowest. However, it seems that errors, too, are likely to be proportional—a 50% error in a war of magnitude 6 is probably about as likely as a 50% error in a war of magnitude 3, though the former represents a much higher absolute number. Under our system of classification, a 50% error would give the same degree of mis-classification in both these two cases and be regarded as an error of equal seriousness. This seems the best approach.

Wars 1820–1949

Magnitude (logarithm of deaths)	Number of deaths	Number of wars
0 to $\frac{1}{2}$	0–3	
$\frac{1}{2}$ to $1\frac{1}{2}$	3–32	not readily
$1\frac{1}{2}$ to $2\frac{1}{2}$	32–316	countable
$2\frac{1}{2}$ to $3\frac{1}{2}$	316–3,160	209
$3\frac{1}{2}$ to $4\frac{1}{2}$	3,160–31,600	71
$4\frac{1}{2}$ to $5\frac{1}{2}$	31,600–316,000	26
$5\frac{1}{2}$ to $6\frac{1}{2}$	316,000–3,160,000	7
$6\frac{1}{2}$ to $7\frac{1}{2}$	3,160,000–31,600,000	2

We have already discussed the accuracy of the figures involved in the calculations of the magnitude of wars. Another similar problem is what casualties to include. There are a range of possibilities which can give very different results. We could include military personnel killed in battle or who died of wounds; or all people killed as a direct result of warfare; or all those who died as a result of the war including the indirect deaths due to disease which can be legitimately attributed to war. The inclusion of disease is by no means a trivial matter as, in earlier times, disease was much more likely to kill a soldier than anything else. In the Boer War, five times as many soldiers died of disease (mainly typhoid) as were killed as a direct result of battle.

Disease also attacks the civilian populations. The influenza epidemic which ravaged Europe at the end of the First World War killed 150,000 people in Britain compared with 750,000 killed in battle, which is not a trivial proportion[16]. The severity of the epidemic may well have been due to the malnutrition and privations caused by the war, though it is hard to be sure of this.

35

Which grouping we take is to some extent arbitrary. What is important is that we are consistent in our selection methods throughout. As far as possible, the magnitudes expressed here include all military deaths, no matter from what cause and, as far as can be judged, all civilian deaths which are directly attributable to hostile action, but not those which are attributable to disease.

If we were to be as accurate as possible, then the war deaths would have to make allowance for the fact that some of the dead would in any case have died from some other cause if the war had not intervened. In the case of military deaths this factor can be ignored, as we are dealing with relatively young and healthy men whose death rate is insignificant compared with the other inaccuracies involved in the figures. In the case of civilian deaths, this factor cannot be dismissed so easily. We might attribute some war deaths to malnutrition, for example. However, the people who are most likely to succumb to this are the very young and, more particularly, the very old, whose chance of dying from some other cause is also fairly high. However, compared with the total figures for the war and the great errors involved, even this correction will not alter the whole picture very much.

Another possibility for inclusion is the number of people who would have been born if their prospective fathers had not been killed. Decisions of what to include and what not to include begin to get very difficult. If the unborn children are included, why not the unborn grandchildren? Why not also the children who would have been born if their fathers had not been away? But if so, do we deduct those who were born in a rush after the fathers returned? In short, the assumptions on which such a calculation could be made get so complicated that it is easier to abandon the quest and make do with the more down-to-earth data which we have.

3 The Analysis of Statistical Hypotheses

As we are discussing the statistical approach to war, it will be necessary to introduce some simple statistical concepts. These, however, are fairly straight-forward and the non-mathematician need have few fears.

Statistics, at least as applied to data, is the business of classifying. Thus we might classify the people in a room at a party by counting the number of people who are more than six feet in height and those who are less, those who are men as opposed to those who are women, those who drink more than one glass of whisky an hour as opposed to those who drink less. But there is no requirement that there should only be two classes into which we divide people with respect to any attribute. Thus we may count the people who drink no whisky, one whisky, two whiskies and so on. We also frequently try and relate two different classifications such as, for instance, body weight and drinking habits, to see whether there is any tendency for heavy drinkers to be in the heavy weight category, in the light weight category, or not to show any significant bias.

Suppose we are at a party at which the only drink is whisky, and we carefully observe the number of drinks each person has. At the end of the party, we make a list of the number of people who drank any given number of whiskies and tabulate the result as follows:

Number of whiskies (x) drunk per person	0	1	2	3	4	5	6	Total no. of people
Number of people drinking x whiskies	4	31	39	16	6	3	1	100

We could then plot it in a diagram as follows:

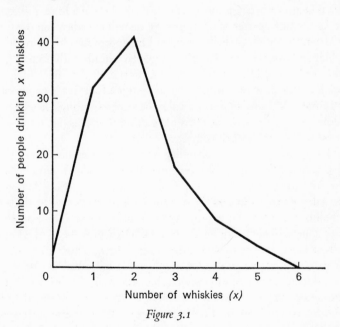

Figure 3.1

Such a table and resulting diagram is called a *distribution*. Distributions play a fundamental role in statistical analysis.

The distribution of people according to their whisky drinking habits is derived purely from observation (or a hypothetical observation—the author did not in fact carry out the experiment); there is no particular theory behind it. Let us now consider the following rather different problem.

Suppose we induce some fanatical devotee of the experimental method to toss a coin four times every day for a year and record the results according to how many heads he got each day. Thus, in his daily diary, there would be one of five entries: no heads, one head, two heads, three heads, four heads. At the end of the year, we want to construct a diagram indicating how many times he got any given result. The question is, can we predict roughly how many times each result will occur in the year?

Let us first consider the case of all heads turning up. To put the question more specifically, what is the *probability* that, on the 12th March, he will get 4 heads. The probability that his first toss of the morning will result in heads is $\frac{1}{2}$. Thus on 'about' half the mornings he will get a head on his first go. If the 12th March were such a day, he would toss the coin again, again with a probability of $\frac{1}{2}$ of it coming up heads. Thus on 'about half' of the mornings on which he gets a head on his first go, he will also get a head on the second go; or, on about a quarter of all mornings, he will get a head on the first two goes. The 12th March is such a day, and he approaches his third trial. On about half of the mornings on which he got two heads with his first goes, he will also get a third head, making the proportion of days on which he gets this result $\frac{1}{8}$. It is now easy to see that he will get four heads on about $\frac{1}{16}$ of the days. As the chance of getting a tail is the same as getting a head, we could have done exactly the same analysis for getting four tails (i.e. no heads) and got the same result: $\frac{1}{16}$ of the days.

Now let us look at the probability of getting three heads and one tail. Suppose we take first the probability of the experimenter getting heads on his first three tosses and a tail on the final toss. We have already demonstrated that he will get three heads on the first three tosses on about $\frac{1}{8}$ of all days. On about half of these days he will get a tail on the last toss. Thus, on about $\frac{1}{16}$ of all days, he will get head, head, head, tail. However, he is asked only the number of heads, not in which order he got them. Thus, for example, he would therefore regard the result, head, head, tail, head as equivalent to head, head, head, tail. We can see that there are four possibilities of just one tail turning up, namely when it appears in the first, second, third or fourth position. By an application of the earlier argument we can see that each of these will occur on about one day in sixteen, so one will turn up on about $\frac{1}{4}$ of all days. The argument is identical for one head and three tails, so now we have the approximate proportion of times on which four of our five categories will appear. As these four categories account for $\frac{10}{16}$ of the days, it follows that the final category of two heads and two tails will account for the remaining $\frac{6}{16}$ of the days. If we now make a distribution of the number entries we predict will fall into each category, we get the following picture.

No. of heads per day	0	1	2	3	4
No. of days	23	91	137	91	23

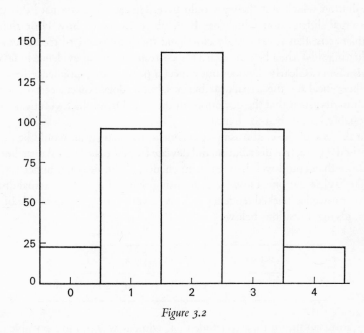

Figure 3.2

This type of distribution is known as the *binomial distribution.*

Now it is unlikely that our dedicated experimenter will have actually got the exact numbers we have predicted for him in the table. It is, after all, a chance matter and it is, in principle, possible, though in practice extremely unlikely, that he would have got four heads on every single day of the year. This ideal distribution, which is predicted on the basis of our postulates about the behaviour of the coin, is known as a *theoretical distribution*, as distinct from the actual observed distribution.

Now the statistician bases an interesting form of reasoning on the preceding procedure. Let us assume that he has a theory about the nature of some chance process. In the coin tossing case we first described, the theory is that, on every toss of the coin, there is an equal chance of it coming down heads or tails. Furthermore, each toss is independent of the preceding tosses, so, for example, it makes no difference on the fourth toss of the day whether the first three tosses were all heads, all tails or any mixture of the two. He then works out a theoretical distribution on this basis. The theory is clear cut in the case of tossing coins, but in more complicated social situations the appropriate theory is by no means so obvious, though the principle is the same. The statistician, having formulated his theory, works out the theoretical distribution which this theory would give. He can then compare this with the actual distribution which has been observed to see how close the resemblance is. If it is reasonably close (and there are standard techniques for evaluating this), then he can regard the correspondence as evidence in favour of his theory. Clearly, he does not expect a perfect correspondence between the theoretical and the actual distributions, but he does expect a certain degree of similarity, such that the deviations of the actual from the theoretical could reasonably be ascribed to chance.

In the case of the coin tossing experiment, the statistician would be rather surprised if the actual distribution did deviate from the theoretical distribution by more than could well happen from chance, as the situation under review is a fairly clear cut one. However, supposing that it did, and the actual distribution showed a marked tendency to move over to the right hand side of the table, giving a result as below:

No. of heads per day	0	1	2	3	4
No. of days	1	17	80	156	101

The statistician might then conclude that, while it was still just possible that his original hypothesis was correct, it was nevertheless rather unlikely, and that, more probably, the coin in question was biased towards heads so that it was not in fact a fair coin. Thus, on the basis of the evidence, he would reject his initial hypothesis.

In the next section, we shall give an example of how Richardson used this mode of reasoning for the examination of the frequency of wars.

In the last example, we took almost the simplest situation we could have had, namely when the probabilities of the two events were equal. The same principle applies, however, even when the probabilities differ. Suppose we had had a die and were interested in the number of times a six turned up in series of four throws done on every day of the year. Here the probability of a six appearing on any given throw is only $\frac{1}{6}$. By using the same style of argument as before, the probability of getting a series of four sixes on any given day is only 1/1296. That is, throwing one's die dutifully every day, one would expect to get four sixes about once every three and a half years—perhaps a surprisingly small number. If we did this exercise for one year, one would expect to get a distribution something like the following

No. of 'sixes'	0	1	2	3	4
No. of days occurring	176	141	42	6	0

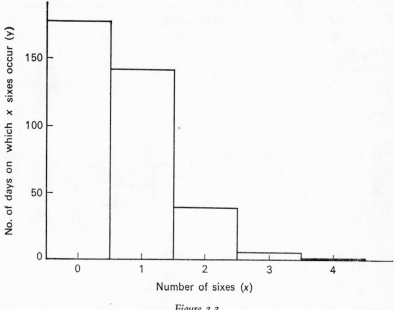

Figure 3.3

This diagram looks rather different from the last. However, in view of the very similar processes used to generate the two different diagrams, it is easy to believe that they are very intimately connected, mathematically. We express this intimate mathematical connection by saying they are derived from the same form of distribution, but the different shapes of the graph indicate that different probabilities were involved.

Different ideal graphs are produced, not only by altering the probabilities involved, but also by taking a different distribution, that is, by altering the underlying assumptions of the problem. Take the following type of case, which is of considerable importance in many studies, including our own. The number of cars which meet with an accident along a given stretch of motorway is a very small proportion of the number of cars which travel along the motorway. Suppose, for the sake of argument, that there is an average of three accidents a week. There will not, of course, be exactly the same number of accidents every week, and we are interested in the number of weeks which will have any given number of accidents. The theoretical distribution of the number of accidents per week is shown below and is known as the *Poisson Distribution*. We get this sort of distribution in situations where there are very many opportunities for an event to occur (i.e. in our example, there are very many journeys on the motorway), but a very small probability of the event (i.e. an accident) actually occurring.

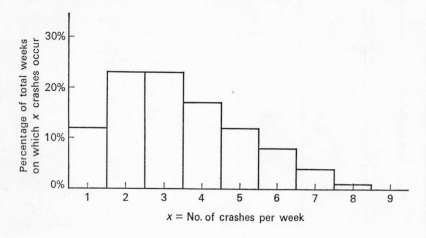

Figure 3.4

4 The Frequency of Wars

Richardson posed the problem of whether we can tell anything about the origin of wars by observing the frequency of their occurrence. As a period of analysis, he took the period 1820 to 1929 which, despite the defects of the information involved, was nevertheless better documented than any other period. Further, he took the wars which had a magnitude of more than 3.5, so the chance of any serious omissions is fairly small. Big events in history, for obvious reasons, are less likely to be omitted from the records than small events. The number of wars of the appropriate magnitude in this period was quite large, namely 110, so a meaningful statistical analysis could be performed.

The first stage in the analysis was to ask how many years there were in which no wars started, how many there were in which just one war started and so on. It turned out that in no year did more than three wars actually start. As he was concerned only with the cause of war and not with for how long they went on, he did not worry about how many were being prosecuted in a year. The table below gives the result of this classification.

The next stage is to think up a hypothesis which would give some explanation for this distribution, that is, which would throw up a theoretical distribution which roughly corresponds to this observed distribution. He advanced the notion that there are a great number of occasions on which wars could occur. However, on only a very few of these does a war, in fact, start. If this were the case, then it would produce a Poisson distribution of years classified according to the number of wars which started during them. Richardson then compared this Poisson distribution with the actual distribution and, as is shown in the table and diagram on page 44, they correspond fairly closely.

The use of this analysis, as is so often the case in the social sciences, is not in what it confirms, which still leaves many questions unanswered, but in that it rules out some possibilities which are by no means self-evidently foolish. Obviously, by standing so far back from the problem, we are severely restricted in what we can do. However, it was only in this way that we were able to make eliminations which would otherwise have remained possibilities.

What does this analysis show? The distribution of the data is consistent with the hypothesis that wars could have occurred on a large number of occasions but actually happened only in a small proportion of possible circumstances, due, presumably, to some chance element or configuration of elements being present. However, although the statistics are consistent with this conclusion, it does not mean that we can affirm it for certain. Other assumptions might have given not very different results.

Perhaps it is more interesting to ask what alternative hypotheses this rules out (or, more modestly, makes appear rather more unlikely). One candidate, a theory of the distribution of wars which is by no means self-evidently absurd, is some sort of cyclic theory. It could be argued that the more wars are fought, the more are likely to be fought because of some brutalising effect. However, when this goes too far, an exhaustion effect sets in, reducing the number of wars started. Such a theory is not borne out by Richardson's statistical analysis as it would have implied a greater number of entries in the years with larger numbers of wars starting than is found here.

Outbreaks of War. 1820–1929. Magnitude 3·5 to 4·5

No. of outbreaks of war per year (x)	0	1	2	3	4	more than 4	Total
No. of years in which x outbreaks occurred	65	35	6	4	0	0	110
Theoretical no. of outbreaks* which 'should' have occurred	64·3	34·5	9·3	1·7	0·2	0·0	110·0

Source: Richardson, *Statistics of Deadly Quarrels.*

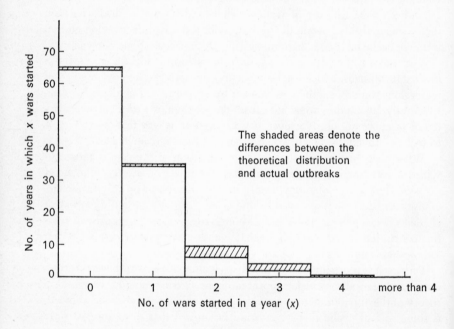

The shaded areas denote the differences between the theoretical distribution and actual outbreaks

Figure 3.5

* Obviously the actual number of outbreaks must be a whole number. The 'theoretical' number, however, need not be, though there is no meaning to the notion of, say, 0·3 of a war.

In fact, the Richardson analysis supports what is a fairly conventional historical view of the causation of war. States, by and large, exist without fighting but, now and again, events take an unusual turn which results in war. It may not be the same turn of events every time, and the Richardson theory is not inconsistent with the view that the cause of each war is unique. A uniqueness theory would, in fact, require a Poisson type process.

Outbreaks of War. A.D. 1500 – 1931

No. of outbreaks of war per year (x)	0	1	2	3	4	more than 4	Total
No. of years in which x outbreaks occurred	223	142	48	15	4	0	432
Theoretical no. of outbreaks which 'should' have occurred	216·2	149·7	51·8	12·0	2·1	0·3	432·1

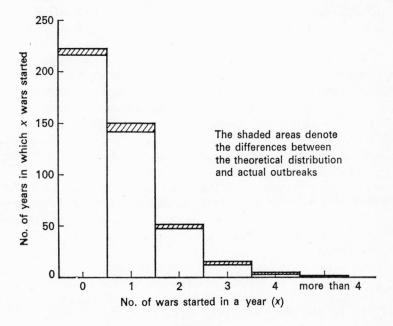

The shaded areas denote the differences between the theoretical distribution and actual outbreaks

Figure 3.6

Richardson applied the same approach to the data collected by Quincy Wright covering the longer period from 1500 to 1931. The data here are less reliable, partly because of the larger number of years and partly because Wright had less of Richardson's care for definition and classification. However, the historical and the theoretical distributions which are given in the table and graph on page 45 show a close correspondence.

5 Mass Data Analysis

Richardson was the pioneer in the collection of statistical data about the international system, and, even more clearly in the statistical analysis of the data. However, a great deal of work has gone on since then, both in the collection and analysis of data. The computer, a machine already referred to with great respect in this book, has made it possible to carry out statistical analyses of large quantities of data which would have been quite impracticable without it. It has completely altered the scale on which statistical analysis can be conducted.

Until relatively recently, there has been a paucity of data on the attributes and characteristics of the international system, both in terms of the actual attributes of the actors involved and the type of behaviour they adopt. The problem is now being remedied in all areas of political science by the various collections of data which are being made, usually on a comparative basis. Associated with data-collection are the data-analysis schemes in which, not merely are the data collected, but there is also an attempt to see what patterns appear (though some patterns are likely through chance alone). It is very much a growth industry in the study of international conflict, and a comprehensive description of what is going on would require a book to itself. We shall discuss just one of the more important techniques of mass data analysis—namely Factor Analysis—and one or two of the more interesting of the very many results[17].

Prior to describing Factor Analysis as such we must go back and describe a more basic statistical concept, that of *correlation*. Two variables are said to be correlated if, on average, they move consistently together, either in the sense that one increases as the other increases, or one decreases as the other increases.

Suppose we take a large group of people and find the height and the weight of each of them. We would find that, on the whole, tall people were heavier than small people. This would not be true of all cases, but there would nevertheless be some pattern in this direction. The two variables would then be said to be *positively correlated*. If two variables move in opposite directions to each other, then we say they are *negatively correlated*. Thus, the number of people watching television on Sunday afternoon is likely to be negatively correlated with the number of minutes of sunshine during that afternoon—the more sunshine there is, the less television watching, and vice versa. Again, it will not be true of every Sunday afternoon—a good programme will attract more people to watch—but in general the proposition will hold. There is a zero correlation if there is no relationship between the two variables at all. Thus, if we were to compare the height of people with their intelligence, then it is unlikely that we would find any relationship between the two.

Now, obviously, there are degrees of correlation. In some cases there are very close correlations between two variables and, given the value of one variable, the value of the other can be predicted with some confidence. In physics, very high correlations of this sort exist. However, sometimes and particularly in the social sciences, all that exist are tendencies. While it may be obvious that one factor influences another, there are clearly other things operating too. We can then extend the analysis and include other variables in it. Thus, in the television example, we can introduce, not only the number of minutes of sunshine, but also the temperature (which in itself is correlated, not by any means perfectly, with the number of minutes of sunshine—it will vary at different times of the year, for example). We can also bring in the popularity of the programmes. The same general principles apply whether we are dealing with one or several variables acting on the dependent variable (the one whose level is to be explained in terms of the others). The more relevant variables we bring in, the more accurately are we likely to be able to predict the level of the dependent variable from observation of the explanatory variables—or, in the jargon of the trade, the less unexplained variance is left. In social affairs, we are very unlikely to be able to explain anything perfectly, but this does not matter unduly. We wish to explain predominant patterns and are not particularly troubled by some deviations from a complete explanation.

The degree of confidence we have in whether a pattern representing some common influence is present or not, depends in part on the number of observations there are. Five observations lying close to a straight line could well come about by chance but a hundred are unlikely to be accidentally arranged in this manner. Large numbers of observations on the behaviour of a set of variables are thus desirable in order that statements may be made with confidence.

That the concept of correlation is widely used in the statistical testing of hypotheses is hardly surprising. However, in the case of a very large number of variables (as distinct from observations, i.e. values for the variables), the technique needs extension. Factor analysis is essentially a correlation technique suitable for situations where there are a large number of variables which are relevant, or thought to be relevant to a problem.

The technique was originally developed for use in psychological contexts. Suppose it is observed that there are various personal attributes which go together, such as verbal ability, ability at solving logical problems in tests, speed of learning new languages and so on. One of these variables, say verbal ability, could be singled out and all the others tested for correlation with it. We would expect the other variables to be highly correlated with this. However, as a procedural device, we could also *invent* a new 'dummy' variable with the property that it is correlated as highly as possible with the set of already inter-correlated observations. This hypothetical variable could be said to be an underlying *factor* which in some sense 'explains' the behaviour of the other variables. In the case we have been discussing, we can invent a hypothetical variable and call it 'intelligence'. Instead, then, of saying that verbal ability is correlated with the ability to learn Russian quickly, or indeed any of the other psychological characteristics which are likely to go together, we may say that verbal ability is highly correlated with intelligence.

The procedure can be approached in a different way when the structure of the problem under investigation is not properly known. Instead of defining the constituents of the factors, one can explore the whole set of variables to see what patterns exist, and extract the factors from these patterns. There need be no prior definition of what goes into a factor, it becomes a matter which is determined by the procedure. It is this sort of procedure which has, in the last few years, been widely used in the analysis of the international system, as we shall go on to describe briefly.

There are obviously dangers and difficulties in this sort of approach. The dummy variable is purely an artefact and, strictly speaking, is nothing more than a statistical convenience for discussing certain types of data when there are large numbers of variables under consideration. However, to stay at such a level of methodological purity gets rather difficult, and it is easier to refer to these factors as if they were 'real' variables, providing it is borne in mind that they are only artificial constructs. This is not too troublesome in the case of factors like intelligence which are obviously created variables, though even here there is the danger of slipping into the habit of saying that high intelligence 'explains' the ability to learn Russian quickly. In fact, intelligence only describes a whole host of attributes which are commonly associated with the ability to learn Russian quickly and does not constitute an explanation in any but the crudest sense.

The behaviour of states, like the behaviour of people, is a very complex phenomenon. There are very many variables which, in some way or another, are relevant to the study of conflict or international behaviour in general. Factor analysis is a means of reducing the situation to some order, and of discerning any patterns there are in it. There are now a number of studies which have used the technique to explore patterns of behaviour, the most important of which is the Dimension of Nations project at the University of Hawaii.

A number of studies have been carried out under the auspices of this project. Different aspects of the study involve different numbers of variables but, to give some sort of feel for the orders of magnitude involved, the Tantner [18] study of the behaviour of nations in the mid-fifties involved 94 variables and covered 82 nations. Not all the variables were available for every nation and, as would be expected, there are a number of missing elements. Another study covering the same number of nations between 1955–57, employed 236 variables. The analysis of such quantities of data would be completely impracticable without the computer, so this form of analysis has been possible only during the last two decades or so with the development and ready accessibility of computers.

The patterns which appear as a result of factor analysis are interesting, both in the amount which a small number explain, and in the nature of those factors which do the explaining. Fifty per cent of the behaviour of the international system can be explained in terms of four factors, that is, it is clustered into four types of behaviour. These are the sets of variables called the 'participation dimension', the 'conflict dimension', the 'aid dimension' and the 'ideology dimension'. This suggests that the behaviour of the international system is structured. If nations were very dissimilar from each other and consisted of random distributions of characteristics, then there would be no such patterns discernible, or rather, chance configurations of patterns would give very weak correlation effects. However, this is not so, and the patterns cannot reasonably be ascribed to chance.

While the factors involved do appear to account for a lot of the variance, the naming of the factors is open to some objection. In the 'participation dimension', which is the leading one, military factors loom quite large. For example, 'many military personnel' appears as a variable in this cluster, though admittedly in a relatively minor place. Similarly, in the 'aid dimension' there appears a variable 'Large ratio of English titles translated to all translations'. It is not clear what this has to do with aid, and it would not normally be regarded as an element involved in the definition of aid. This is a genuine difficulty in the interpretation of factor analysis. The clustering of variables is discovered by the techniques, and some description of each of the clusters seems called for. However, they may well involve variables which do not fit together under any conventional heading. So, although for practical reasons it is helpful to apply conventional descriptions to unconventional sets of factors, this can be misleading as the subtle re-definition of terms can involve serious misunderstandings.

One of the most impressive and startling results which has come out of the factor analysis studies is the fact that there is only a slight positive relationship between foreign and domestic conflict[18]. In general, one would expect that nations which were prone to violence internally would similarly be prone to external violence, but this is not true. Notice that this does not, of itself, refute the proposition that nations troubled by internal violence go in for foreign adventures to unify the country behind them; but it does make it clear that this is not such a widespread phenomenon as the concentration on one or two instances might have suggested. This proposition has also been tested using time lags—for example, to see whether domestic violence leads to foreign violence a year later. The relationship here seems a little stronger, but it is far from dramatic. Pending refinements of classification, the result seems to hold, despite running counter to prevailing conventional wisdom.

The use of factor analysis represents a big step forward in the 'stamp collecting' stage of the development of the discipline. This is the business of collecting, sorting, classifying data and perhaps using it to test some plausible hypotheses. This is an important phase in the development of a theory. Darwin looked at vast numbers of specimens, and Freud examined large numbers of patients, while formulating their theories. The facts can often suggest the theory, just as the theory can often suggest the facts to be looked for. Factor analysis is predominantly in the first category.

chapter four

The Theory of Games

1 The Theory of Games

The theory of games is the not altogether appropriate name of a body of theory which prescribes how 'rational people' should make choices in some rather stylised conflict situations. The theory has many ramifications. However, the aspects of it with which we are immediately concerned are its implications for the classification, and its use in revealing the basic structure, of certain forms of conflict, stripped of their confusing details.

The theory of games is not as concerned with amusements as its name might suggest. Indeed, the applications of the theory to military strategy chill the heart and, if pondered too deeply, appal the imagination. A game, in fact, is simply a conflict situation which is carefully and unambiguously defined, and not necessarily a game in any of its more commonly understood senses. Admittedly it is often convenient to describe the Theory of Games in terms such as card games, but the theory is by no means exclusively related to parlour games. The theory of probability owes its origin to the analysis of gambling in the eighteenth century, but the word 'probability' was wisely substituted for the word 'chance' in the nineteenth century, thus giving the analysis greater social respectability. No doubt a similar social uplift awaits the Theory of Games.

The subject first came to prominence in 1944 with the publication on *The Theory of Games and Economic Behaviour* by John Von Neumann and Oscar Morgenstern[19]. The discussion, as its title suggests, was in terms of economics, when not in terms of games such as poker. However, the revolution in economic theory, which at the time was assumed by some to be the likely result, never materialised, and its effects on economics, though significant, have still been relatively modest, certainly as compared with the expectations. The theory had been developing slowly during the interwar period, one name of significance being that of the French mathematician Emile Borel. Von Neumann, too, was working on the problem at the time, and to him must go the main share of the credit for the theory in its present form.

In its pure form, the theory of games is simply a branch of pure mathematics. From a particular set of mathematical postulates, a rich, interesting and sometimes surprising set of mathematical conclusions were derived. It is this mathematical structure which is, strictly speaking, the theory of games. To be useful to the social scientist, however, these conclusions have to be interpreted in terms of what goes on in the real world, and this has not always proved easy. For instance, the hoped for description of a competitive economy in terms of the theory has not so far proved very rewarding.

Essentially the theory is prescriptive and not descriptive. That is, it recommends a course of action, defined as rational, and then goes on to describe the consequences of such conduct. It is open to dispute as to whether the recommendations are, in fact, rational—there are various different possible definitions. The theory tells us what would happen if the particular behaviour rules recommended are followed, and it is still of importance whether or not these rules are accepted as rational. A descriptive theory, on the other hand, describes what people actually do, whether the action is wise or foolish. It is a description of the world as it actually is, not as it might be if certain forms of behaviour were adopted. Now, it is possible that a prescriptive theory might also turn out to be a descriptive theory, and a useful first attack on many problems of behaviour is to assume some form of rationality, but to be prepared to abandon it if and when it becomes untenable.

Strategy is a prescriptive study—that is, the study of how to achieve various objectives in war—and, possibly for this reason, the theory of games has seemed appropriate and been popular amongst strategists[20]. It should be clearly recognised, however, that, if it is used in strategy or in any other prescriptive sense, the theory (if it is an appropriate theory) only tells one how best to achieve a given set of goals. Whether those goals are good or not is a question outside the scope of the theory as such, though it should not be beyond the concern of the theorist.

The development of the theory of games since 1944, has been slower than would have been expected. A depressing fact is that a book published in 1957—*Games and Decisions*, by Duncan Luce and Howard Raiffa,[21] which was an expository work on this and associated theories (and, incidentally, a model of what an expository work should be) is still a good exposition of the field at this time. There have, of course, been developments, but the book has by no means been superseded by the work done in the years succeeding its publication. As the theory is still not a very satisfactory tool for the social scientist, despite the enormous amount of work which has been done on the subject by extremely talented people, this suggests that it lacks some crucial requirement which would make it an effective tool for the analysis of human conflict behaviour.

However, there are important uses for the theory of games. There is little doubt that the formal statement of conflict problems has clarified the nature of conflict, and it is some of these clarifications which it is the purpose of this chapter to convey. Further, there is a great deal of work which has clearly been inspired by the theory of games, even though purists refuse to acknowledge it as such because it does not fit into the framework of a deductive, axiomatic theory[22]. Game theory has inspired much experimental work on how people actually behave in various gaming situations, and it has also suggested the description of conflict situations in game theory form. While an analysis of conflict according to the strict precepts of game theory leaves us little wiser on how people really behave, the formulation of the problems in broader game theory terms is of great help. Indeed, if the theory of games is considered to include the formalisation of gaming problems, then this, the child of the pure theory of games, its more rigorous but less worldly father, has added considerably to our understanding of the problem of conflict. It is only the hope of finding the solution of the problem of conflict by the simple application of a neat mathematical theory which has been disappointed.

2 The Zero Sum Game

To explain some of the basic concepts of the theory of games, we shall consider as simple an example as can be formulated, which still preserves the characteristics of a game. This form of game is one of a class called *zero sum games*, by which it is meant that, whatever one player wins, the other loses so that the total benefit of the two players is zero—hence the name. The reader should not be put off by the simplicity of this game, nor its remoteness from international conflict situations. We are attempting to show the basic elements of the situation which will be of help in looking at more complex problems.

Suppose Albert and Billy are playing a game in which each is given three playing cards. Albert has the ace, two and three of some suit of cards while Billy has the Jack, Queen and King. Both can choose which one of his three cards to put out. They play the cards simultaneously so that they both operate in ignorance of the other's move. Suppose that Albert puts out the ace and Billy the Jack; then the rule of the game specifies that Billy pays Albert £3. Suppose, however, that Albert had played the three, and Billy still the Jack. The rules now specify that Albert pays Billy £3. As is clear from the table below, there are nine possible pairs of cards which can be played out in this game. We specify who pays who, and how much, for each of the pairs by means of the table below, which is referred to as a *pay-off matrix*. A positive number indicates that Billy makes the payment to Albert and a negative number indicates that Albert makes the payment to Billy.

		Billy's move		
		Jack	Queen	King
Albert's move	Ace	3	2	4
	Two	4	1	0
	Three	−3	−2	5

Numbers represent £ units

The question is: 'How "should" Albert and Billy, as two rational men, play this game?' At first sight, there may seem little to be said. Suppose Billy plays the King, Albert would do well to play the three and get £5, whereas he would get only £4 if he plays the ace. However, if Billy plays the Jack, Albert would be better off playing the ace. As he has no knowledge of Billy's intentions, what can he do?

Let us assume a particular rule of choice, and then we shall show that the particular rule we have taken has, in fact, a great deal to be said for it. The rule which we advocate to Albert is: examine each of the three choices you have available, and see what would be the outcome if Billy were to counter this in the way which is worst for you. (This is, of course, the outcome which which is best for him.) Then choose the card which corresponds to the best of these worst outcomes. In other words, find the lowest number in each row of the pay-off matrix and then select the row which has the highest of these lowest numbers. This is known as the 'maximin' rule, that is, the rule of maximising the minimum. The obverse, in a situation when a player is bound to make a loss, is known as the 'minimax rule', which is that of minimising the maximum loss. It is convenient to refer to both rules together as the maximin rule, which is a perfectly natural extension of language if we are willing to interpret a loss as being a negative benefit. The maximin rule of conduct plays a fundamental role in the theory of games.

A parallel rule is given to Billy. We can make the situation clearer by extending the matrix with a further column in which is given the worst pay-off in each row for Albert, and another row in which the worst pay-off for Billy is given. (Remember that a high positive number is bad for Billy as it represents his payments out.)

If Albert operates the rule suggested, he will play the ace, which will mean that the worst which can happen to him is a gain of £2; Billy, using the same rule, will play the Queen, so that the worst result for him is to pay out £2. We see, however, that this 'worst result' is exactly what occurs. The ace and the Queen are played, and Billy pays Albert £2.

		Billy's move			Albert's lowest gain (the row minimum)
		Jack	Queen	King	
Albert's move	Ace	3	2	4	2
	Two	4	1	0	0
	Three	−3	−2	5	−3
Billy's lowest gain (the column maximum)		4	2	5	

This might seem a rather depressing rule of conduct, but think of any of the alternatives. Suppose that Albert and Billy play the game a number of times. Suppose also each decides that the best method of play is to assume that his opponent's last move will be the same as his next one, and to make the optimum response. Both start off by being naïve optimists, Albert playing his three in the hopes of getting £5, while Billy plays the Jack in the hopes of getting £3. Billy is delighted as his hopes are fulfilled, but Albert is disappointed and shifts to playing his two, making Billy pay out £4. Billy now shifts to the King and there is no payment, Albert goes to the three and receives £5, and so Billy moves back to the Jack and gets £3, after which we can repeat the process. We shall thus get a cycle of four different results with payments to Albert of − £3, + £4, £0 and £5, giving an average per time of £1½. Now Albert can see that, no matter what Billy does, by playing the ace consistently, he can always get at least £2, and perhaps more. Thus, he will adopt this course in preference to the naïve alternative. However, Billy can also carry out this mental exercise and realises that it in Albert's best interest to play the ace. If he assumes that Albert is a 'rational' man, then he will choose the best strategy against the ace which is, of course, the Queen. So we end up with the prescription we originally urged.

The essence of this scheme is that it assumes that the rival is a prudent man. If he is not, then the maximin policy might not be the best. However, to avoid the rather tricky problem of rationality, with its confusing philosophical overtones, we shall describe the maximin policy as being a 'prudential policy'. Whether 'rational' or not, it is undoubtedly a rule of prudence; and in this case, though not in all possible cases of human decision, it is the only discernible prudent way to act.

The value given by the selection of the ace and Queen can be seen to be the minimum value in its row in the matrix and the maximum value in its column. This is the only element in the matrix with these properties, and its value is known (not unreasonably) as the '*value of the game*'. When such a point exists, it is known as the *saddle point* of the matrix. However, there is no certainty that the minimum row value and the maximum column value will coincide, as is shown in the following (absurdly) simple two choice game.

		Billy's move	
		Queen	King
Albert's move	Ace	1	0
	Two	0	1

In this case, there is no saddle point and the two players can see nothing to choose between the two alternative strategies.

A device has been suggested, however, whereby this difficulty can be overcome. Consider again the situation when the players are playing a sequence of identical plays using this particular pay-off matrix. Previously we suggested that the players should both use the same strategy on each occasion. Now let us consider the possibility of their using different strategies on different occasions.

Let us suppose that, using the simplified pay-off matrix, Albert plays the ace half the time and the two half the time. If he were to do this according to some fixed rule, such as alternating the two, then Billy would soon get the hang of this and be able to play consistently so as not to lose anything. However, if Albert were to play the two cards an equal number of times but in a haphazard manner, then Billy would have no basis for making a choice between his two strategies. If he played the Queen consistently (assuming for the moment that Albert does not take advantage of this), then half the time he would lose one, half the time he would lose nothing, and the average loss would be $\frac{1}{2}$. The same would be true if he played the King all the time. We have thus invented a new strategy for Albert which consists of playing his ace and his two an equal number of times in a random manner, giving an average pay-off of $\frac{1}{2}$ against any action of the opponent. We can represent the pay-off matrix of this new derived game as on page 57.

By playing this new strategy, Albert can ensure for himself an average payment of one half. This is called a '*mixed strategy*'.

However, if Billy still sticks to either the Queen or the King consistently, Albert will spot this, abandon the minimax strategy and gain a payment of 1. To guard himself against this, Billy must also play the Queen and the King on

		Billy's move	
		Queen	King
Albert's move	Ace	1	0
	50% Ace 50% Two	$\frac{1}{2}$	$\frac{1}{2}$
	Two	0	1

a half and half basis in a haphazard manner, in the same way as we recommended to Albert. This will mean that each of the four possible combinations of Ace-Queen, Ace-King, Two-Queen and Two-King will occur on a quarter of the occasions, and the average payment made by Billy to Albert will be $\frac{1}{2}$. The resulting pay-off matrix will look as below.

		Billy's move		
		Queen	50% Queen 50% King	King
Albert's move	Ace	1	$\frac{1}{2}$	0
	50% Ace 50% Two	$\frac{1}{2}$	$\frac{1}{2}$	$\frac{1}{2}$
	Two	0	$\frac{1}{2}$	1

The middle point of this matrix is a saddle point. Any deviation of either player from this mixed strategy can be taken advantage of by the other, so this is the prudent position which we would recommend to both players.

The concept of the mixed strategy has been explained in terms of a series of games in which the players employ different strategies on different occasions, but it can be applied even if the game is to be played on only one occasion. The pay-off resulting from a mixed strategy is really an average of the possible pay-offs. Even if the game is to be played only once, this average can be taken to represent the 'rational hope' of playing such a mixed strategy, although the final result will be either one or zero. This 'rational hope' (more properly referred to as the 'mathematical expectation') can be interpreted as the price an insurance company would be prepared to pay Albert for the right to play the game once.

The insurance company would be willing to pay him $\frac{1}{2}$ of whatever units were in question—minus, presumably, a little allowance for profit. Taking this abstract notion of mathematical expectation and using it as if it were a genuine entry in the game is thus not too far fetched.

The result obtained by Von Neumann which really makes the theory of the zero sum game interesting is that, by using this sort of mixed strategy, any zero sum game between two players, no matter what the form of the pay-off matrix, has some pair of strategies which will yield a saddle point. That is, there is always a 'safe' way of playing a game, where 'safe' is defined in this rather particular sense.

To get this impressive formal result (whether it is of practical application is, as has been said, in some doubt), it is necessary to be able to specify actual numbers in the matrix. These numbers we shall call *utilities*. However, in the problems which we shall discuss and in which mixed strategies are not involved, the numbers we put in are for illustration only and the argument does not depend on precise quantification.

Apart from the unrealism of the games described, there is still the issue of the interpretation of a mixed strategy in the single play game. Albert wants to conceal from Billy which of the two strategies he is going to use. He further wants Billy to think that he is equally likely to use either. Now, the best way of concealing one's intentions from a rival is to conceal them even from oneself. This is perfect security, and is, of course, what happens if a choice is determined by a chance device such as by tossing a coin. However, this is peripheral to the major argument. The crucial issue is not that Albert chooses his strategies according to some random device, but that, as far as Billy is concerned, he might as well be. In the instance discussed, the impression which Billy would wish to convey is of being equally likely to make either choice. If the probabilities had been one in ten, then the impression should not be one of complete uncertainty, but rather one of 'probably going to use one strategy but not quite for sure'. Precisely how the selection is made is not very important.

An obvious point concerning either of these two games is that, if Billy is bound to lose, why should he be willing to play them? He may, of course, be forced to play, but a theory which applies only to games which one of the players is forced to play does not seem entirely satisfactory. There are two relevant replies. First of all, exactly the same theory applies to a game in which the pay-offs to the two players are equal to some constant positive sum, so that both can win. Consider the following game, where each of the entries in the pay-off matrix is represented by a pair of numbers in brackets. The first number represents the pay-off to Albert and the second that to Billy. The sum of the numbers in any of the brackets comes to 20, and this form of game is not surprisingly referred to as a *constant sum game*.

		Billy's move		
		Jack	Queen	King
Albert's move	Ace	(13, 7)	(12, 8)	(14, 6)
	Two	(14, 6)	(11, 9)	(10, 10)
	Three	(7, 13)	(8, 12)	(15, 5)

By applying the same maximin rule of choice in this case as we did in the first game we analysed, we find that the solution is for Albert to play the ace, and Billy to play the Queen, with the result that they get 12 and 8 respectively. For the purposes of analysis, however, the two games are identical, the zero sum game being merely a special case of the constant sum game in which the pay-off to Albert plus the pay-off to Billy equals zero. It is clear that it is in the interests of both players to participate in any positive constant sum game, in which the saddle point involves gains for both. The critical characteristics of the constant sum game (whether zero sum or not) is that the sum of the pay-offs to the two parties should be equal irrespective of which pair of strategies are played.

The second reply is that we can look at this, not just as a procedure for recommending to Albert and Billy how to play, but as a method for either Albert or Billy to determine whether to play at all. If Billy is asked 'Would you like to play this game?' he would be wise to look at the prospects of winning by 'playing', that is analysing, a hypothetical game. In our zero sum examples he would decline the offer, as he would be bound to lose. He could not have come to this decision without having some sort of theory with which to analyse the game, and the theory suggested here seems to be a good one for the purposes. It is not useless simply because it is not actually practised in play.

These have been objections to the theory as applied to this very simple game. Another class of criticism refers to the whole concept and asks why should two people, whom we are presupposing to be in some sense rational, trouble to play a game which is so absurdly trivial? People do play very simple games (like noughts and crosses), but only when they are very young or very bored. The theory is of any practical use only if it can be extended to cover much more complex situations. In principle this can be done, but in practice it is extremely difficult because of the enormous number of options which have to be considered.

3 'Prisoners' Dilemma' and 'Chicken' Games

Two very simple and stylised non-zero sum games have played a considerable part in the analysis and classification of conflicts. It is not suggested that any (or at least many) real life conflicts have such simple structures as these games. They do, however, form a basis for classification: by looking at these simple games, we can get some insight into the nature of more complex conflicts.

The basic story of the Prisoners' Dilemma to which the problem owes its name runs as follows. Two men in possession of guns are picked up by the police. Though they are doing nothing at the time, the police have a strong suspicion they were earlier involved in an armed robbery, though they cannot prove it. The two prisoners are therefore taken into separate rooms and each is made the following offer, in the knowledge that the other is being made the same offer: If you confess to the armed robbery and your partner does not, then we will speak up for you in court and you will get only one year in prison. If you confess, and your rival also confesses, our plea for leniency will carry less weight and you will get five years. However, if you do not confess and your partner also does not confess, you will not be convicted for the robbery—but you will both get two years for carrying arms. If you do not confess but your partner does, you will bear the brunt of the punishment and get ten years.★

We can arrange the alternatives available to each participant, and the results of the alternatives, in the matrix below.

	Not confess	Confess	
Not confess	(2, 2)	(10, 1)	
Confess	(1, 10)	(5, 5)	

Entries in the matrix represent years in prison

The dilemma in the situation is obvious. Clearly both of the participants should confess as, no matter what the other one does, each will have done better for himself in this case. However, this results in both of them getting 5 years in prison whereas, by refraining from confessing, they could both get only two years and be better off. If they cannot communicate with each other, they end up with a mutually undesirable solution which could have been bettered for both of them.

We can express this in a slightly more general way. Let us assume that

★ This procedure is not allowed in Britain. The legal realism of the story is, in any case, of low order.

Albert and Billy are once more playing a game, this time with a pay-off matrix as follows where the payments are in pounds.

		Billy's move	
		Queen	King
Albert's move	Ace	(4, 4)	(1, 6)
	Two	(6, 1)	(2, 2)

It is clear, on inspection, that this pay-off matrix describes what is basically the same situation as the prisoners' dilemma, for whereas in the prisoners' dilemma a small number was preferred to a large number, in the money game the reverse is true.

The essential problem remains the same. Albert, as a prudent man, would clearly be well advised to choose the two. Indeed, whatever Billy does, it is always to Albert's advantage to play the two. If Billy played the Queen, playing the two would give Albert £6 instead of £4, while if Billy played the King, Albert would get £2 instead of £1. Almost any rule—prudence, rationality, or anything else except altruism—would suggest the playing of the two. Likewise, Billy should play the King, for he will do better compared with playing the Queen no matter what Albert does. If both parties follow this obviously sensible advice, they will each get £2. By not being sensible they could have had £4.

The reason for regarding this as a dilemma, or even a paradox, is obvious. Both players act in a rational manner, but they end up in a position which could be improved on for both of them. Both could have been better off if they had selected the other strategy. Individual rationality in this case does not lead to social rationality, which is a disturbing conclusion and violates many intuitive preconceptions of the consequences of individual rational conduct. Intuitively one feels that, if everyone is motivated only by his individual self-interest and acts according to some precepts of rational conduct, then either all, or at least some, of the actors should be better off. However, this case shows that this is not true. Two people acting according to rules of individual self-interest *both* fail to achieve as much according to this criterion as if they had violated such rules.

The prisoners' dilemma model can be used to provide a simple picture of some types of international conflict. Suppose we have two hostile countries wondering whether to go in for some expensive new form of defence system. The anti-missile missile systems which the U.S. and U.S.S.R. are actively considering are a good instance. The situation is such that, if neither have such an anti-missile system, then there is a stalemate. If both have a system, then there is still a stalemate, so neither have a strategic advantage. However, the acquisition of an anti-missile system is very expensive, so that the stalemate with such systems is worse for both parties than it would be without, because of the high costs involved. If one country has the system but the other has not, then the strategic advantage is substantially weighted in its favour, and we assume that this advantage is worth the cost of acquiring it.

For the sake of clarification, let us put some numerical values to the advantages and disadvantages of various courses of action, recognising that these numbers are for illustration and commit us only to very weak forms of measurement. Let us suppose that the strategic gain to a country due to having an anti-ballistic missile missile system when the other does not have one is 250 national interest units. However, if the position is reversed and it is the other side that has the system, the strategic loss is seen as —250 national interest units. However, the cost in terms of economic resources of acquiring the system is 100 national interest units, so the net gain of being in the strategic lead is 150 units. If both obtain the system, the strategic balance is arrived at but both are paying a cost of 100 units. Thus we can build up a pay-off matrix as below which can be seen to be essentially the same as the Prisoners' Dilemma. The *status quo* is regarded as zero.

	Not carry out programme	Carry out programme
Not carry out programme	(0, 0)	(—250, +150)
Carry out programme	(+150, —250)	(—100, —100)

Instead of assuming that this is a Prisoners' Dilemma which is just played once, we can conveniently amend the situation and consider it as a continuing condition, where the participants enjoy the pay-offs for each year the situation in question continues. Let us assume that they are currently at the *status quo*. Both are trying to work out what they should do. Suppose that country A decides to go in for building anti-missile missiles. This will become known to B at some time and he will recognise that, if he does not imitiate a similar programme, he will be at a strategic disadvantage. There is therefore an unambiguous gain in also carrying out a programme—from the threatened —250 to —100, which is worse than the original position, but is, at least, better than being in the strategically disadvantageous situation. The end result will be — 100 for both parties and both will have made themselves worse off. The initiator will, however, have seen this possibility for himself and will recognise that attempting to start the programme will end up by making both sides worse off. This may deter a potential initiator as he can see the mutually damaging result. This is unfortunately not certain, though, because the period of gain before his rival has replied might seem worth the ultimate loss. Further, he might be afraid that his rival would introduce the anti-missile missile system so as not to be caught out in the losing situation. To study these questions would require an elaboration of the model which would make it more complicated (though still, as it happens, perfectly susceptible to analysis). The simple model indicates that the system should not be built—but the complications cannot be ignored. It is to the credit of the simple model that it clarifies the form that these complications and modifications of the model should take.

The problem of disarmament or tension reduction can be looked at in much the same way. Suppose two countries have a high level of arms directed against each other. Both parties would like to move to a lower level, which would still leave their relative strategic positions the same but would relieve the strain on their economies. However, for one party to cut arms unilaterally would leave it strategically weak to an extent which would not be regarded by its rulers as justifying the economic saving. Let the strategic gain of being armed on one's own be 100 units and the drawbacks of being unarmed 100 units. The cost savings are fifty units, so the net drawback of unilateral disarmament is 50 units. The zero *status quo* base is now the armed situation in the bottom right hand cell of the matrix. Starting from this, we can build up the following situation:

	Arms reduction	Arms *status quo*
Arms reduction	(50, 50)	(— 50, 100)
Arms *status quo*	(100, — 50)	(0, 0)

Posing the problem in this form exposes the bare bones of the logic of the situation. If A decides to reduce his arms he would lose, not gain, in National Interest unless B did likewise. B, however, would have no particular incentive to follow by reducing his arms as it would also lower his National Interest from the bonus figure given by A's reduction. More pessimistically, then, we conclude that the non-cooperative position also has some strong elements of stability, in that neither side is likely to make the move necessary to get them to the stable cooperative position.

This highlights, but no more, the reason why unilateral disarmament moves are very rare. Disarmament and arms control negotiations are normally concerned to try to get over this hump by making all parties reduce arms together, meaning that they move from the bottom right to the top left-hand box without a transition through the other corner boxes, which the injured parties would never accept. Even this formula is rarely successful.

'Chicken' is the other game we can look at as a stylised formulation of a conflict. The generalised pay-off matrix consists of two acts, cooperative and non-cooperative, as in the Prisoners' Dilemma, but the pay-off matrix, given below, differs in the significant respect that the bottom right hand entry is lower for both parties than any other.

	Cooperate	Non-cooperate
Cooperate	(100, 100)	(50, 150)
Non-cooperate	(150, 50)	(0, 0)

Suppose both parties are currently at the cooperate position. A sees that he can make a gain by going to the non-cooperate position. Furthermore, this position is a very strong one for A, in that it would not be in B's interest to dislodge him from it. Unless motivated by revenge, B would do best to shrug his shoulders philosophically and accept the reduction in his interest. The desire for gain on the part of A is intensified by his dislike of loss for, if B makes the non-cooperative move first, A will similarly find himself in a loss position he can do little about. Both parties are then in a situation where it would be highly beneficial to them to 'pre-empt' the other, that is to act first in an aggressive manner. If one succeeds, we get to one of the mixed situations. However, if they both act together, they will end up in the mutually harmful bottom right hand cell. Unlike the Prisoners' Dilemma, the Chicken game does not have any great measure of stability in the cooperative position.

A hypothetical situation meeting the Chicken game's conditions is when two countries are eyeing an intervening territory which both see an advantage in having and a disadvantage in the other having. However, if one country invades before the other, there is little the passive country can do except wage war, which it regards as more harmful even than the other country's possession of the territory. The incentive is for both parties to move as quickly as possible, but, if they do so simultaneously, war is the result, with a loss to everyone.

The Prisoners' Dilemma and Chicken games can be used to illustrate that there are two forms of deterrence. Deterrence is rather roughly defined as one party making it clear to an opponent that, if he acts in certain ways, then the deterrer will punish him by inflicting some cost which will make the overall consequences of the act too expensive to be attractive. Mutual deterrence occurs when both parties threaten each other with 'Don't do it or else . . .'. Now, the act of punishment may itself benefit the deterrer or it may harm him. The first of these positions is illustrated by the Prisoners' Dilemma, while the second is illustrated by the game of Chicken. We give examples of the two below.

Deterrence 1. (Prisoners' Dilemma)

	Do nothing	Act (or punish)
Do nothing	(0, 0)	(−10, 10)
Act (or punish)	(10, −10)	(−5, −5)

Deterrence 2. (Chicken)

	Do nothing	Act (or punish)
Do nothing	(0, 0)	(−10, 10)
Act (or punish)	(10, −10)	(−20, −20)

Clearly, the Prisoners' Dilemma form of deterrent is much more credible than 'Chicken' deterrence. In type 1 deterrence, the punisher actually gains by punishing as compared with submitting (though by less than his loss due to the original initiation of the action). However, in type 2 deterrence, he can only lose by punishing and must be motivated by other considerations not included in the matrix, such as a desire for revenge or a belief that he must act to preserve the norms of the social system, even at the cost of personal disadvantage.

To illustrate this point further, we can put the issue of nuclear deterrence into game form. We can simplify the choices open to the participants to two: use nuclear weapons or do nothing. As it does not affect the basic argument, we assume the consequences of a second strike attack (that is, one after the opponent has already carried out a nuclear attack) as being the same as for a first strike. Let us put in two possible entries in the bottom right-hand box.

	Not attack	Attack
Not attack	(0, 0)	(−1,000,000, +100,000)
Attack	(+100,000, −1,000,000)	(−900,000, −900,000) (−1,200,000, −1,200,000)

If the top entry in the bottom right hand box is the one which is seen as appropriate, then the game is one of Prisoners' Dilemma. It implies that an attacked country derives benefit (if only in the satisfaction of a desire for revenge) by itself carrying out the attack. If this is thought to be the case, then the credibility of deterrence as a means of avoiding nuclear attack (though not necessarily other disadvantageous courses of action) is high. If the deterrence situation is of type 2 (the lower entry in the bottom right-hand position in the matrix), the deterrer has to convince his opponent that he will act against his own interests to carry out the punishment. This configuration of the matrix is by no means unreasonable. A country which has just suffered nuclear attack might be helped by its attacker, if only out of a desire to exploit it. Further, the extra fallout in a world already heavily impregnated would harm the second attacker as well as its victim. On the other side, the only benefit is in the satisfaction of getting revenge, so a 'Chicken' picture is just as plausible as a 'Prisoners' Dilemma' picture. But this means that the successful application of the theory of deterrence involves convincing one's opponent that the deterrer will act irrationally and against his own self interest should the need arise. This is a curious but important implication of the theory of deterrence, a concept which appeals to the hard headed.

The aim of using these games, at least as presented here, is to clarifying ideas. Behaviour in the Prisoners' Dilemma is likely to be very different from that in the Chicken game, so, by analysing conflicts in terms of these and other single paradigms, we can get some insight into their basic structure. Rarely, of course, do situations present themselves in terms of simple two-choice alternatives, but this does not always matter as far as analysing the basic structure is concerned and, in any case, we can complicate the models if this seems appropriate and useful.

chapter five

Bargaining and the Theory of Games

1 The Question of Information

If the two participants in a non-zero sum game can agree to co-ordinate their actions, they can normally obtain some outcome which compared with others which might have occurred, is to their mutual benefit. There are two problems involved here. First, there is the question of to what degree they are able to co-ordinate their policies, which is clearly a question of how well they can indicate to each other what actions they will take. Secondly, there may be several different outcomes which could be chosen, all of which are better than those occurring without co-ordination, but some of which are relatively better for one party than the other. The activity whereby two contending parties decide between themselves what actions to take, when some are better for one than for the other, is called bargaining. When it is done by explicit verbal communication, we refer to it as negotiation. The two problems inherent in the bargaining process are, therefore, that of communication in order to co-ordinate actions appropriately, and that of agreeing on what is the appropriate co-ordination of actions.

First, we shall tackle the problem of communication. Let us consider the Prisoners' Dilemma situation, discussed in chapter 4, which was represented as below.

		Billy's move	
		Queen	King
Albert's move	Ace	(4, 4)	(1, 6)
	Two	(6, 1)	(2, 2)

We discussed how, if Albert and Billy were prudent men and unable to communicate with each other, Albert would play the two and Billy the King, and neither would be very satisfied with the result. The obvious thing for them to do in this situation is get together and agree to play the ace and Queen respectively. In this simple situation, there is no real problem in deciding what bargain should be reached, as there is only one alternative which both find better than that which results from a purely competitive situation. There is a problem of communication, however, and one which it is useful to solve, as the ability to get together clearly improves the situation quite considerably.

Suppose that, having made an agreement with Billy, Albert suddenly has qualms in case Billy did not intend to keep it. Billy, by cheating, could come out very well. Albert is now back in the old dilemma: 'Billy might cheat, and I'd be in a bad way—so perhaps I should cheat to guard against this; in any case I'd be better off doing that . . .', and so on. Thus the simple act of negotiation does not necessarily solve matters. It depends on how far each party to the negotiation believes that the other will carry out his promises. For the exchanging of information to be really effective, the agreement has to include some provision for policing it in order to ensure that it really is followed. This is unnecessary only in cases where the word of the negotiator can be completely relied on. In domestic matters, many important agreements are backed by some legal arrangement which enables a person to take sanctions against a defaulter. Such devices are necessary, or at least useful, to ensure that negotiations over such things as financial and commercial arrangements are, in fact, meaningful.

The problem of enforcing agreements made in negotiation is clearly seen in disarmament discussions. In the last chapter, the problem of disarmament was posed in terms of the Prisoners' Dilemma. Both parties agree they would be better off with a lower level of armaments, but they both know that the rival would profit by cheating. The problem, then, is to devise appropriate methods of making sure that cheating does not take place. The largely abortive efforts to achieve disarmament in the post war world have been concerned as much with methods of policing as with the actual content of the agreement. They have been complicated by the fact that policing methods have other costs to the inspected party, in that extra military information is likely to be acquired. The danger that a disarmament inspection agreement would give the United States an intelligence bonus seems to have been one of the reasons for the Soviet Union's reluctance to have on-site inspections for nuclear tests.

So far, we have considered only the problem of explicit communication. However, a great deal of communication of intention goes on without any spoken or written statements being made. This happens when countries (or people) have completely ruptured the negotiating channels, as is the case today with U.S.A. and China (with the exception of some semi-surreptitious meetings in Poland, and possibly some completely surreptitious meetings about which, clearly, the author is not informed). Communication still takes place through public speeches which the other side will read, through third parties, and by means of signs such as the movement and use of armed forces. Military sign-language is used, even when there is explicit communication, but when there is doubt as to whether the statements are believed.

Unfortunately, indirect communication, and particularly military sign-language, is much less efficient than a verbal communication which is believed. It is cruder, so nuances are less easily discernible, and it is prone to misunderstanding. The difficulty of distinguishing between the curtailment of military activity which is intended to convey the message 'I am willing to negotiate' and that which is meant to say 'I am weak and almost beaten', is notorious.

Suppose we again take the Prisoners' Dilemma as played between Albert and Billy, assuming this time that they play the game several times over without being able to communicate directly. After a few losing runs, Albert begins to get tired of what appears to be mutual destructiveness, and wants to communicate that he is willing to play his ace in return for the playing of the Queen. The rules of the game forbid him to talk to Billy. He can, however, play the ace for a few goes, knowing that he will lose by doing so, but hoping to communicate to Billy his willingness to be co-operative. Billy may or may not take the hint. He may refuse because he wishes to extract the most from Albert's desire to co-operate, or he may fail to understand the message which is being conveyed. Implicit communication is usually less efficient than explicit communication, largely because of the greater likelihood that the nature of the message will be misunderstood. This sort of problem is discussed in greater detail by Schelling [20].

Communication is often a mixture of explicit and implicit messages in cases where it is difficult to know whether to believe the explicit statements. This is common in warfare and takes the form of some statement such as that a nation will not cease fighting unless certain conditions are met. The United States has made several statements of this sort in connection with Viet Nam. However, those who are supposed to take note of the statements may not know whether to believe them or not; so, in order to attempt to convince them, some action is taken, such as escalating the bombing, which is intended to confirm the explicit message. However, it might not be at all obvious to the North Vietnamese that this action was supposed to be a preliminary move towards peace proposals. Nor, indeed, was it very clear to many others, including the author. Military sign-language is not an efficient method of communication.

It is clear that the business of communication is complex, and we have therefore considered four categories: no communication, implicit communication, explicit communication where there is doubt about the truth of the negotiators' statements, and explicit communication where there is either adequate policing of the agreement, or faith in the word of the negotiator. There is also the hybrid class of explicit communication reinforced by implicit communication. Of course, it is possible to classify the possibilities in more detail but, for our purposes, this grouping is quite sufficient.

2 'Fair Bargains': the Arbitrator's Problem

The development of the theory of bargaining has gone along two paths' which have sometimes intertwined and sometimes even been mistaken for each other. The first question is, 'What is a "fair bargain"?' Bluntly posed like this, it is ultimately an ethical question. However, it can be posed rather more neutrally. Suppose an arbitrator is given the task of suggesting the form of an agreement between two contending parties. He will have some idea of the characteristics that the final agreement ought to have, which might be an amalgam of what is 'fair', and what would have been the result if the two parties had fought out their disagreement by whatever ways were open to them. We shall examine one set of 'arbitrator's rules' in a rather stylised situation, and see what their implications are. The second question to be considered is 'What sort of agreements do people actually reach in specified bargaining situations?' Obviously these will not always be 'fair' in any normal, or even extended, sense of the term. This problem is examined in the next section.

Let us restate the bargaining problem in another diagram which, to some extent, telescopes the issues we have considered hitherto. First let us consider a Prisoners' Dilemma problem with the matrix as below

		Billy's choice	
		Queen	King
Albert's choice	Ace	(2, 2)	(0, 3)
	Two	(3, 0)	(1, 1)

Now, let us construct a diagram in which we measure Albert's utility up the vertical axis and Billy's utility along the horizontal axis. We can represent the four possible outcomes of the game as points on this diagram, namely M, N, P, and Q. Furthermore, we can join up the points with the lines indicated and argue that, by appropriate mixed strategies, we could achieve any point within the area bounded by the lines. Thus, the point R would be the result of Billy using his first strategy, and Albert using his first and second strategies in a fifty-fifty mixture.

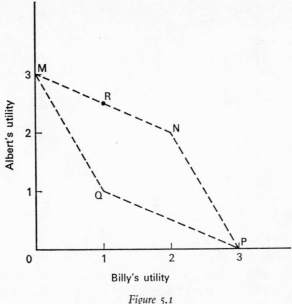

Figure 5.1

For the sake of the analysis, let us consider a game with more possibilities. For simplicity, we shall simply represent it as a set of utilities without actually specifying which acts produce the outcomes. Suppose, then, that we have a situation in which it is possible to achieve any point in the area bounded in the diagram below (Fig. 5.2) by the two axes and the curved line. This area we shall call the 'bargaining set'.

Let us suppose, for convenience, that some provisional agreement has been reached, giving utilities represented by point P. Now, this result could be bettered for both of them by any agreement which lies to the North-East of this point. They should therefore find some new agreement to supersede that at P. This argument applies to any agreement not actually on the North-East boundary of the bargaining set. However, once on the boundary, a problem arises, for any movement on it is to the advantage of one contestant, but at the expense of the other. Albert will aim for a point as high as possible, while Billy will aim for a point as far to the right as possible. This is the essence of the bargaining problem. There are sets of outcomes over which the two parties are in direct conflict, while a failure to select one of these points means, normally, that both suffer. The bargain concerns those possibilities, which can be achieved by agreement, above and beyond those achievable by unilaterally deciding policy.

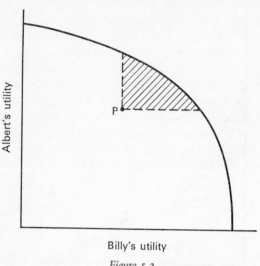

Billy's utility

Figure 5.2

There have been various efforts to formulate a theory of where an agreement point 'should' lie. Most of them imply discussion between the parties, but others require only a more limited degree of communication. We shall pose the problem, as we did earlier, as that of the arbitrator who wishes to suggest an appropriate agreement, and who sets off by proposing that it should have some general characteristics. We shall discuss one procedure, which is illustrative of the general *genre*. It was developed by J. F. Nash [23], and is discussed by Rapoport [24], and, in greater detail, in Luce and Raiffa [21]. Whether one is willing to adopt Nash's scheme or not depends on the extent to which one is willing to accept Nash's 'rules for negotiators'; it has no absolute validity as a prescription for the 'proper' solution of bargaining problems.

Nash's rule for a fair bargain seems, at first sight, to be completely arbitrary. He suggests that we should take the set of utilities of the two parties, multiply the members of each pair together, and then select that outcome as best which gives the highest number. The immediate reaction is that any other combination would do as well. However, Nash justifies this recommendation by demonstrating that it follows as the logical consequence of assuming that an agreement should possess four characteristics. The first of these is rather technical. It is that any bargain should be independent of the utility scales adopted for the participants. The zero point in any utility measure is arbitrary, and the solution of the bargain must not be affected by this essentially irrelevant feature. The second characteristic is that, if the alternatives and their pay-offs are symmetrical for both parties (as in the Prisoners' Dilemma case considered earlier), then whatever rule is adopted should give an equal division to both. The third characteristic is that the solution should be on the boundary of the bargaining set, and not be such that there is a point with a better pay-off for both parties. These last two characteristics, taken together, suggest that, in the prisoners' dilemma case discussed earlier, the solution should be the (2, 2) point. These three characteristics are very innocuous, and it is hard to imagine that anyone is going to dispute any of them very seriously. The final one, though by no means obviously unreasonable, is rather less immediately compelling. We illustrate it by reference to the diagram below.

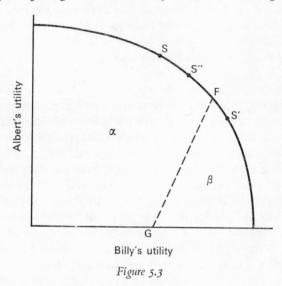

Figure 5.3

Suppose we have a bargaining game which has its outcomes in the area α, which is bounded by the axes, the broken line FG, and that part of the curved boundary between F and the vertical axis. Let the solution of this game be the point S. Now consider an extended game in which the pay-offs can consist of all the points in the area α, plus the points in the area β. It is conceivable that the solution of this extended game could be a point such as S' in the new area. Such a situation would be acceptable. However, if the solution of the extended game is found to be one of the points in the original area, then this point must be the original solution point. Thus, the inclusion in the game of the set of points β must not shift the solution to any point S''. The intuitive justification for this requirement is quite plausible, as can be illustrated by a simple example. Let Albert have a stock of apples and Billy a stock of bananas.

They are haggling over how many apples Albert should give to Billy for some of his bananas, as both would feel better off if they had some of each. Suppose an outsider comes in and alters the game by making the offer that, if they both agree to forgo their stocks of apples and bananas, they can have a good dinner at a restaurant. One of them is unwilling to accept this added possibility in the game as a solution. The bargaining rule posited then insists that this offer should not affect the final bargain which is concluded in the apple-bananas exchange. This requirement is more stringent than the earlier three, but by no means totally unacceptable.

Now, Nash's rule of regarding as a solution the point where the product of the utilities is a maximum meets all four of these requirements in all cases. The really surprising thing is that Nash proved that his rule is also the *only* one which will always meet these requirements. The result is readily interpreted only in stylised situations, but, within its context, it is rather remarkable.

This rule for a negotiator as to how to produce a bargain, though theoretically intriguing, might seem to be merely a curiosity. However, it can also be shown to give the same result as that which would emerge if a particular form of bargaining procedure were adopted. Suppose the arbitrator were to approach his problem by using a rule which would indicate when one party should make a concession, instead of starting from the other end and stating what characteristics the final bargain should have. If, for instance, Albert has said he will settle for point A, giving a utility to himself of a_1, and to Billy of b_1, while Billy has said he will settle for B, with utilities respectively of a_2 and b_2, the arbitrator could take the view that, in some sense, his function is to maximise over-all utility. Initially, let us assume that the bargain has to be settled at either A or B and not at an intermediate point.

An appropriate way of achieving this over-all maximisation is for the party whose relative utility loss is the least to concede to his rival's demand, as the rival's gain will outweigh his own loss. Now, a relative utility loss to Albert in terms of the diagram can be represented as $(a_1 - a_2)/a_1$. Thus, the condition for Albert to concede to Billy's demand is that $(a_1 - a_2)/a_1 < (b_2 - b_1)/b_2$. This* can be re-arranged to read $a_1 b_1 < a_2 b_2$, which is in the form required for a decision on the basis of Nash's rule. Thus, if either A or B had been the Nash point, then, using Nash's rule, it would be selected as the optimum solution. However, there is no reason whatever why one of the two demand points should be the Nash point. In many problems, some intermediate compromise position between the two demands is quite possible.

Thus we need a more general rule of concession. Let the arbitrator state

* The sign < can be read as the phrase 'is less than'.

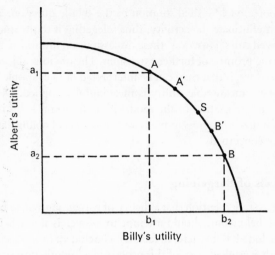

Figure 5.4

this to each party as: conceded if, and only if, your opponent's relative utility loss is not less than your own.

Suppose Albert agrees that, because of his lower relative utility loss, he should make some concession. He will not go all the way, but agrees to go to A'. The problem is not yet resolved, but the same sort of procedure can be repeated, the party with the lowest utility loss making the concession. In this way, a suggested solution point is always abandoned if the product of the utilities is less than that of the point with which it is being compared. Thus, a series of concessions is examined until some point S is reached such that there is no point with utilities which have a product greater than $a_s b_s$. But this point is also the Nash point. Thus the rather surprising conclusion emerges that the concession rule, which has no apparent connection with the Nash rule or the principles which yield the Nash point, nevertheless produces the same answers. The two principles reinforce one another and compel one to take seriously what at first sight appears to be a completely arbitrary solution point.

This is not the only sort of concession rule that a negotiator could adopt. It is, however, a very reasonable one, and one which might well be adopted. The fact that we have two apparently independent and certainly different 'reasonable procedures' which both yield the same point gives added weight to the Nash bargain as being, in some sense of the word, 'reasonable'.

The procedures which are considered under the heading of 'fair' bargains do not, of course, yield a final solution to the whole question. Such procedures will not eliminate the activity, thus relegating it to the simple application of approved rules. However, these discussions do illuminate the problem and hold out the promise of further extensions. The obvious objection to these forms of procedure, is that they can be interpreted only in simple and stylised situations, where measurable utility is meaningfully applied. Developments needed in the interpretation of the model in useful terms—this is, of course, the area which needs progress in many of the aspects of conflict analysis with which we are concerned.

3 The Process of Bargaining

The most interesting question that a theory of bargaining whose basic purpose is to describe behaviour, should attempt to answer is not where a bargain *should* be concluded, but where, in fact, it *is* concluded. In this section we shall describe a rather crude theory of this process in a hypothetical situation.

Let us consider two countries that are unfriendly towards each other, and are indulging in hostile acts such as the restraint of trade, restricting the moves of each other's nationals in their territory, and so on. They are not, however, at war with each other. The relationship which exists between the U.S.A. and U.S.S.R. comes into this category. By reaching agreements on specific matters such as trade, they can both achieve benefits. Now and again, one of the powers accentuates the hostility, and they bargain in a more tense and mutually disadvantageous atmosphere, from which, however, both parties are hoping to improve their over-all position when the tension is over. It is this sort of process which we shall endeavour to fit into a theoretical framework. For heuristic purposes, it is, perhaps, easiest to think of this in terms of trading relations between two hostile countries.

Suppose that the dispute takes the form of one country insisting on exclusive rights in one fishing area, and the other contesting this. Each side is harming the other; one, perhaps, by keeping the rival's fishing boats out of the contested area by force, and the other by refusing port facilities. An attempt to find some mutually acceptable compromise will be made, and a number of different possibilities are readily imagined. There is also a range of further hostile activities—perhaps even violence—that could be carried out, and these would aggravate the problem. In other words, tone party could *escalate* the conflict in the hope of thereby achieving a stronger bargaining position, and either a quicker or a better final settlement.

The argument can be represented on the diagram below as a dispute between two countries, Crim Tartary and Paflagonia. We assume that countries, like individuals, have some notion of 'utility', though, in the case of countries, it is more usual to refer to this utility as 'National Interest'. For convenience, we shall assume that, in some form or other, this national interest is, in principle, measurable. Similar concepts are used in economics in discussing what proportion of a country's resources should be invested, in order to get a higher national income at some future date, at the expense of consumption at the present time.

At the opening of our analysis, Crim Tartary and Paflagonia are fighting at a level which gives them national interests represented by the point I. We shall assume, initially, that neither side thinks of escalating the conflict beyond its present level.

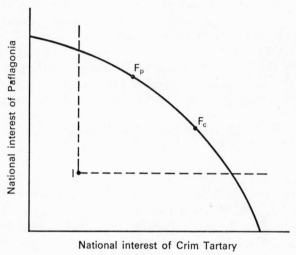

National interest of Crim Tartary

Figure 5.5

Paflagonia and Crim Tartary have made 'final offers' of F_p and F_c respectively. It is not our purpose to inquire how this state of affairs has come about —we shall inquire only what results from it. We notice that, as F_c is above I, it would be better for Paflagonia to choose F_c than to stay in the present position, if for some reason it became absolutely impossible to do anything else. Likewise, F_p is to the right of I, and so would be preferred by Crim Tartary to I. Suppose, for the moment, that the bargaining situation is restricted and that the conflict can be ended only by going either to Paflagonia's final offer or to Crim Tartary's. We can pose the following questions: under what conditions does Paflagonia hold out for its own best offer, and on what conditions does it 'surrender' to Crim Tartary?

We can provide an informal and intuitive answer to the question by supposing that Paflagonia wishes to get the best average level of national interest possible over the whole of the period of warfare plus that of the subsequent bargain. Paflagonia's chief negotiator has choices at any given moment of time. Either immediately concede to Crim Tartary and take their final offer, thus making some gain over his present position; or he can hang on until Crim Tartary surrenders thus, after some delay, making a rather larger gain. The longer it is before Crim Tartary's negotiator is expected to make his concession, the less attractive does hanging on appear. We can presume that there is some point in time such that, if Crim Tartary were not to make this concession until after that date, it would pay Paflagonia to surrender to Crim Tartary immediately; while, if Crim Tartary were to surrender before that date, it would be to Paflagonia's advantage to await this surrender. Now, of course, Paflagonia can only estimate when Crim Tartary will surrender. As time passes, Paflagonia's guess about when Crim Tartary will surrender will probably change. Initially Paflagonia's negotiator might be optimistic and assume that there would be a fixed date. However, if as time goes on, and Crim Tartary remains apparently unwilling to surrender he may get more pessimistic.

The effect of this can, perhaps, be most easily seen in an example. Suppose Paflagonia thinks that Crim Tartary will surrender in 12 weeks' time and has worked out that, providing Crim Tartary concedes within 15 weeks, it will pay them to hang on. After 8 weeks, Paflagonia's negotiator's view about Crim Tartary may be unchanged—he thinks that Crim Tartary will concede at the original date, which is now 4 weeks away. This strengthens his determination to hang on, for he always analyses the problem from the current date. This means that it is worth his hanging on for another 15 weeks, which is, of course, 8 weeks ahead of the original dead-line for profitable concession. After 12 weeks, however, Paflagonia's man has become more pessimistic. His original estimate has been proved to be wrong, and no signs of surrender are coming from Crim Tartary. He advances the probable date of Crim Tartary's concession by 3 weeks. After 16 weeks of warfare, he has become more pessimistic still and adds a further 8 weeks to his estimate of the date of his opponent's concession, bringing the total estimated warfare period up to 23 weeks—16 gone and 7 to go. Notice, though, that he still hangs on, for it will still pay him to wait for this concession. If his initial estimate had been 23 weeks to concession, he would have surrendered then, and will be cursing himself for not having done so. However, he did not, and he now wants to make the best of the current situation, stoically resigning himself to the unfortunate past. After 20 weeks of warfare, his pessimism has become acute. His rival is still showing no signs of weakening and is trumpeting his determination to fight to the end. Paflagonia's negotiator regretfully concludes that it will be 20 more weeks before Crim Tartary gives in, and therefore decides that it would be more profitable to give in himself to Crim Tartary's demand. It would, of course, have been better to have given in at the beginning of the battle, and Paflagonia pays the consequences of the miscalculation.

A similar sort of picture applies to Crim Tartary's negotiator who, likewise, estimates when he thinks Paflagonia will give in and acts accordingly.

In view of the guesswork which goes on, it is quite possible that, at the beginning of the negotiations, both think they can force the other into a position which, at the moment, he will not consider. The one who first becomes so pessimistic about the expected time before concession that he thinks that it is no longer worth while continuing the fight, gives in and accepts his rival's last offer.

Most agreements end in some sort of compromise between the demands of the two parties rather than in the complete capitulation of one of them. This can fairly easily be fitted into the model. Suppose that Paflagonia's man thinks that Crim Tartary will capitulate in 8 weeks if he sticks out for his last offer. As far as Paflagonia is concerned, this means staying at war for a further 8 weeks and thereafter getting the utility represented by their last offer. However, there are some offers which are a little worse from their point of view but which, if accepted immediately by Crim Tartary, would give just as good an overall pay-off, because there would be no initial period of warfare loss involved. If the Paflagonian delegate thinks that Crim Tartary would accept such an offer immediately, then he will try his compromise agreement.

A compromise becomes more likely when both parties are getting pessimistic as to when the rival will concede. If both think the rival will surrender in a short time, only minor concessions will appear worth while, and these may be insufficient to satisfy the rival. If, however, they are both pessimistic, they will both be ready to make substantial concessions and these may well meet with mutual agreement.

To fit the notion of escalation into the theory is fairly easy. If one side decides that, by escalating the conflict, he can induce the other to accept his terms more quickly or, alternatively, to accept less favourable terms, then he will do this. An escalation might be the arrest of the rival's trawlers if they put into the contestant's port. He has to allow for the fact that, if he does escalate, the rival will probably respond to this by also taking further hostile acts. However, even allowing for retaliation, it is sometimes possible for an escalation to be beneficial. The analysis, however, proceeds exactly as it did before and the picture is not fundamentally altered. In diagram 5.6, it simply involves a move from P to P', from where the analysis proceeds as before—one side, however, must have hoped, whether correctly or incorrectly, that this would improve his ultimate position.

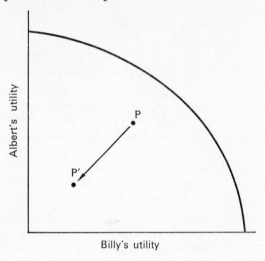

Figure 5.6

This theory is simpler when put in terms of a relatively narrow dispute, but the general principle obtains even when applied to more complex situations. The relationship between the U.S.A. and U.S.S.R. has been one of considerable but varying tension ever since the birth of the U.S.S.R. This came to dominate the international scene after World War II. Reductions in tension can come on many fronts, and the two countries occasionally strike bargains, to their mutual advantage, on one of these fronts. It seems very unlikely that the possibilities are by any means exhausted. From time to time, the situation deteriorates as the result of a deliberate act such as that which precipitated the Cuba missiles crisis. The aim of this was, presumably, to improve the Soviet position. However, there was a miscalculation and the net effect of the crisis, due to the American response, was probably not what had been anticipated by the Soviet Union—though, in the judgement of many, the final result was that both of the principal parties involved were better off than before they started. However, the actual interpretation one puts on particular incidents in the relationship between the U.S.A. and U.S.S.R. is not the issue here. What is relevant is that the relationships can be described in terms of bargaining theory.

4 Bargaining as a General Form of Conflict

The model represents a rather generalised bargaining situation, in the sense that the process is viewed as being temporary and one in which the parties carry out actions with the aim of securing satisfactory permanent end positions. We shall argue that a number of very different types of conflict can be interpreted within the same sort of framework, though some of the differences are as illuminating as the similarities. However, not all forms of conflict can be described as bargaining situations and we shall deal with these first.

The two forms of conflicts which do not fit very readily into this bargaining framework, are firstly, games in the everyday sense of the word (as distinct from the technical meaning used in this book) and, secondly, 'threat conflict'.

In games such as football (of any variety), card games, races and so on, people compete under strictly defined rules. Any consequences or prizes are meaningful only when interpreted in the context of the game. Thus a prize for winning a race is paid only if the race is run, and the race itself is not one of many different ways of deciding on the distribution of the prize money. As a duel also has some of the characteristics of an everyday game, it is necessary to add to the definition that it is played for the entertainment of someone—whether the players or the spectators.

The second form of conflict which cannot be categorised neatly as a bargaining situation is threat conflict. The most interesting form of threat conflict in the present context is arms races. In these, the various parties competitively build up their armaments, but there is no obvious definition of a winner nor is there a clear-cut method of forcing the opponent into a bargain, after which the armaments can be reduced again. They can more naturally be viewed as a set of manoeuvres which are conducted in the face of some other threatened conflict (i.e. a war) so that, if the war takes place, each party will be in what they consider to be a good position for winning. The war itself (as we shall argue) is something of a bargaining situation. Thus the arms race is not, in principle, carried out for its own sake, but because of its relation to another potential conflict. Some arms races approximate to a form of bargaining situation: if one party secures dominance over another, then it may be able to force concessions just by threatening war. However, even here it is the conflict that might ensue which brings about the agreement (See Chapter 9 for a further discussion of Arms Races).

Now let us turn to bargaining wars. We shall compare three types of conflict with each other—total wars between countries, limited wars between countries, and industrial strikes. All these have three characteristics in common: they are regarded as temporary situations (though sometimes long-lasting, nevertheless); both parties aim to force their rival to accept an agreement which they would not have accepted before the period of conflict (in total war the 'agreement' is the virtually complete subjection of the loser); and the period of conflict imposes costs on both parties. Thus, if the final agreement could be predicted at the beginning of the conflict, it would be in everyone's interest to go there immediately. This does not exclude the possibility that some of the members of either party might benefit from the war.

We shall discuss a few of the characteristics in which the different types of conflict agree or differ. At the end of the section are listed various characteristics and how the types of conflict fit into them. This tabulation should not be taken very seriously in that it is too crude, and different instances of each type of conflict have different characteristics. Further, it contains the author's subjective judgements and legitimate issue can be taken with at least some of the entries. The purpose of the classification is to suggest the type of question which may be asked, rather than to propose particular answers.

First, we should distinguish between two forms of hostile activity—escalation and fighting. Escalation means moving the conflict onto a more costly level. In industrial conflict, this might mean calling a strike; in limited war, it would mean carrying the war to a new area or using a type of weapon which, though it had previously been technically practical to use it, had hitherto not been employed. By fighting, we mean hostile acts which do not increase the level of the conflict. Thus, ordering a particular air raid is fighting, whereas ordering air raids to begin in a previously limited war is escalation. The division between escalation and fighting in total war is not very clear, though one might regard the opening of the second front in the second world war as escalation.

This points to a difference between industrial strikes, on the one hand, and violent wars on the other. In the first type of conflict, there is no fighting in the sense that, once the conflict has reached a given level, no more decisions are needed except about further alterations in the level. Each act of hostility, such as the refusal of a particular man to work on a particular day, follows from the general decision to strike, and requires no individual decision to be taken. However, hostile acts in a violent war all require decisions to be taken. The act of capturing a particular farm house does not follow inevitably from the general decision to fight a violent war in a particular area, but is a result of a fresh decision on its own.

Now let us turn more directly to the bargaining model. We divide the aspects of bargaining into four general groups:—

1. Negotiations and information. During a period of conflict, negotiations can be carried out with the aim of reducing the level of the conflict. They provide a flow of information (not always reliable) about the concessions which the two parties might make; without them, a possible and mutually satisfactory agreement might be delayed, just because of ignorance of each other's views. Attitudes to negotiations vary markedly in the different kinds of conflicts. In total war, any suggestion of negotiation is often regarded as treasonable, while, in a commercial dispute, negotiations are not only acceptable but are often pursued with vigour.

2. The status of the final offers. In the model, we assumed that the final offers made before an escalation would still hold during the heightening of the conflict, and that worse offers would not be substituted. This seems common in strikes, for instance. However, in some conflicts, the last offer is revoked as soon as the conflict begins. During total war, demands are pushed up far beyond the pre-war demands and sometimes to absurd levels. Limited war may provide an intermediate case. Related to this point is the attitude of the disputants during the conflict to the losses already sustained. They may take the 'economic' point of view, simply wanting to get the best they can out of the existing situation and letting the losses already endured be forgotten. Alternatively, they may adopt the policy to trying to make the rival 'pay for his aggression' (as, in the circumstances, it would doubtless be called). The Treaty of Versailles which followed the first world war is a clear case of this. The last offer which was made before the conflict started is therefore withdrawn.

3. The parties to the conflict. The theory was constructed in terms of two hostile parties. This is commoner in reality than is sometimes supposed—of the 91 wars ending between 1820 and 1939, in which more than about 3600 were killed, 42 were between just two nations. In total war, such as the last two world wars, many countries were involved. Admittedly the participants were drawn up into two sides, but the interests of the members of the same sides diverged, and their relationships were by no means always smooth. A model in which each side consisted of several more or less independent decision-making units would have to be considerably more complex than that discussed here. Limited war may be even more complex: not only may there be many parties involved in the conflict, but just who is involved and the extent to which they are committed may be obscure. The war in Viet Nam is a good instance of this. The applicability of the model depends on the cohesion of the alliance as, in the model, each side is a single decision-making unit. A tightly bound alliance might approach this, but a loose alliance brings some significant

Characteristics	Total War	Limited War	Industrial Strikes
1 Conduct of negotiations during conflicts	Not conducted —hostile attitude	Varies—often attitudes to negotiation are hard in early stages but soften as conflict progresses	Continued
2 Information about opponent's potential compromises	Very low	Low, though may improve as conflict progresses	High
3 Attitude to losses already incurred in a conflict	Hardening of attitudes in favour of 'winning'	Sometimes written off, sometimes not	Written off except in very prolonged and serious conflict
4 Position of final offer before the conflict began	Withdrawn	Often modified	Maintained
5 Relation between nominal and actual Obscure aims of the conflict		Often the same but sometimes diverge	Usually the same. Less so in 'wild-cat' strikes.
6 Inter-unit solidarity when opposing sides consist of several decision taking units (countries, unions, etc.)	Often low	Medium	Usually high when applicable
7 Intra-unit solidarity (e.g. within a country)			
(a) Extent	Very high	Medium (low)	Usually high
(b) Development through conflict	Stable	Variable	Fairly stable
8 Degree of knowledge concerning opponents' reaction to escalation.			
(a) Whether reaction will take place	Not applicable in present framework	Often low	High
(b) Extent of reaction	Do.	Often low	High (few alternatives)

deviations. A possible extension of the model would recognise that each decision-making unit represents an amalgam of different interests, which may have substantially different views on the conflict. Some groups in a country may oppose a particular conflict, even during its worst phases. This happens in commercial conflicts. There is a great difference, in different forms of conflict, between the unity within each of the groups for which the decision-making bodies are acting.

4. Knowledge of opponent's reactions. The knowledge of what sort of reaction to expect from an opponent varies radically in the different types of conflict, and probably also between different conflicts of the same type. Three problems are raised in connection with this issue: first, will an opponent react; second, what will be the extent of the reaction; and third, how long will the opponent continue his hostile posture? In the case of a strike, the first two questions are answered unambiguously— the strikers know that the employer will cease to pay wages. One or other party will make a false estimate of how long the other can hold out (or even, on occasion, how long it can hold out itself) but extreme errors are likely to be avoided. To examine these three questions for the case of violent war would require a more clear-cut concept of escalation than has yet been formed, and so we shall not attempt to provide answers here. The case of limited war is where there seems to be the maximum doubt as to what an opponent's reaction will be. There is frequent doubt even about whether the opponent's reaction will be hostile or conciliatory. It is interesting to note that this does not deter many observers from expressing very dogmatic views on the precise reaction to be expected to any move.

The table opposite presents a summary classification and comparison of the different forms of conflict mentioned. The classifications are too crude for serious analysis—'limited war', in particular, covers a multitude of sins, and counter examples can be found to almost any entry in the table. However, as generalisations, they will provide suggestions for a useful and relevant set of questions.

chapter six

The Theory of Alliances

1 The Problem of Alliances

There are approximately one hundred and thirty-four countries in the world, the precise number depending on the definition of 'country'. We might wonder, for example, whether to include Liechtenstein on the grounds that its diminutive size means that it lacks some of the essential attributes of a national State. Less plausibly, we might exclude China as it is not a member of the United Nations. These hundred or so countries do not determine their relationships with other States in complete isolation from one another, but form alliances of varying degrees of strength and, on certain issues, decide policy together. The word 'alliance' is not used here in any technical sense, and still less in any legal sense; it is taken to mean any sort of amicable co-ordination of policy. Thus we get strong alliances like that between Britain and the U.S., and weaker friendships (here also called alliances) between, for instance, Britain and Sweden, where there are fewer formal agreements. It is unlikely that either Sweden or Britain would threaten the other with military sanctions in any dispute.

An alliance usually excludes some members who, in principle, could have been in the alliance but who are not. We could conceive of an alliance in which every country was a member, and it would have some of the attributes of the type of alliances we are discussing. The United Nations was conceived as such an alliance, though the exclusion of China has made this aim non-operative. However, such alliances have other, different characteristics, and we shall be more interested in those which not only include members, but also exclude others. Countries excluded from an alliance may form one or more of their own.

There are many different sorts of alliance, but we are basically interested in those in which some military component is involved. This may be a strong agreement to help out the other members in time of war, or it might be a very weak understanding not to do various things which could be interpreted as hostile.

The structures of international alliances vary very much, and all sorts of patterns have appeared at some time in history. Countries sometimes involve themselves in fairly general alliances with each other, in which they more or less agree about their relationships with other States. Complete agreement is unlikely. The post-war British and U.S. relationship has been fairly close and, by-and-large, there is agreement on policy. Nevertheless there are divergencies, such as over the recognition of China, trade with Cuba, and, particularly in the nineteen fifties, over the policy to be adopted concerning the Middle East. However, there is a degree of willingness to give mutual support over and above the formal agreements which are laid down under such organisations as NATO, which would distinguish the British–U.S. relationship from, say, the British–French or British–Indian relationships. There are also alliances, either formal or informal, which commit countries to helping others under certain specified situations such as invasion, but which do not commit them to a more general support of each other. Obviously, the borderline between an agreement and an alliance is a thin and wavering one. One could almost define an alliance as existing when there are some sufficiently large number of explicit or implicit agreements.

Another classification of alliances is between the hierarchic as against the egalitarian alliance. A completely hierarchic alliance is one in which the leader of the alliance virtually tells the rest what to do; in a completely egalitarian alliance there is no discernable leader. The Eastern European alliance appears, during the late forties, to have been quite close to a completely hierarchic alliance, though it is now a little looser. The Western alliance, though more egalitarian, nevertheless had a clear leader in the United States, whose influence on the behaviour of the alliance was clearly much greater than that of anyone else. Pure instances of either type are inevitably hard to find except, perhaps, for short periods of time.

Apart from the different types of alliance which can exist, there are also different patterns of alliance structure into which the world can be divided. At one limit, there can be a Hobbesian 'Each against all' state of affairs, but this is not a likely pattern. Alternatively, the world could be divided into two alliances such that every country is a member of one or the other—this is a pure case of what is described as the tight bipolar system. Again, a picture of the world in, say, the early nineteen fifties is that it consisted of two fairly tight alliances plus a large residual category of countries, the neutrals, who were in neither alliance but who were also not in any real alliance with each other (though there were several sub-alliances within the neutral group, of course). Yet another possibility is of having several alliances in existence together with a bevy of neutrals. The present position of the world seems to fit into this pattern, which is, of course, extremely complex. We have little reason to mourn the passing of the 'hard' cold war days, but the tight bipolar system of which it was a member had the merit of being easier to understand[28].

The purpose of a theory of alliances is to try to see why alliances form in the way they do, form in the sizes they do, and if possible why they break up when they do. These problems can be treated as aspects of the theory of games. So far, we have examined the theory of games in terms of just two participants—that is, as a two-person game. Once more than two participants are introduced, it is necessary to discuss the various possible patterns of alliances or coalitions which might arise among them. This business of determining coalition formation is a major aspect of the three or more person game. It has even been suggested, in view of the relatively disappointing prospects for the application of the rest of the theory of games, that its ultimate importance will be seen to lie in its contribution to the theory of alliances, though such a view is, at this time, a pure speculation.

The difficulty with any theory of alliances is that the problem can become remarkably complex, as the number of ways in which even a few nations can combine is legion. Suppose that ten countries can form any number of alliances (including the one where each alliance consists of one single member) and that the alliances can be of any size. The total number of patterns of alliances possible under such circumstances is 115,975—or 115,974 if we exclude the single case of all being in one alliance!

We can make the problem a little less fearsome if we break it down into a set of more restricted problems. Let us name the ten countries simply by letters of the alphabet, A, B, C, D, E, F, G, H, I, and J. Let us also distinguish between an *alliance structure* and an *alliance pattern*. An alliance structure we shall define as a breakdown of the total number of nations into a specified number of alliances, with specified numbers of members in each alliance. Thus, one possible alliance structure of the ten nations would be one alliance of four members and two of three members. This would be distinguished from another structure consisting of three alliances, one of two members, one of three members and one of five members. However, in an alliance structure, we do not specify which countries have to be in which alliance, so a set in which the first alliance consists of AB, the second of CDE and the third of FGHIJ is regarded as having the same structure as the set IJ, FGH, and ABCDE. However, these last two sets do have different alliance patterns, for a pattern takes into account not only the structure but also the membership of each alliance.

Suppose the ten nations form a bipolar world; that is, every nation is a member of one of two alliances. In this case there are five possible alliance structures, namely 1 against 9, 2 against 8, 3 against 7, 4 against 6, and 5 against 5. However, there are 511 different alliance patterns, which is a large number. Thus, in the structure 1 against 9, there are 10 different patterns— A against the rest, B against the rest, C against the rest and so on.

A more realistic, but slightly more complex problem arises when there are two antagonistic alliances with a third bloc consisting of neutrals. The neutrals are not strictly an alliance in the sense that they have a common policy, but they are distinct from the members of the other alliances—they are a sort of residual alliance. Suppose that countries A and J form the core of the opposing alliances. The remaining countries can go into alliance with A or J or join the neutral camp. We shall assume that it is possible, but not necessary, for either A or J or both to be left alone, and also that there will be at least one neutral. In this situation there will be 14 alliance structures and 1,221 alliance patterns.

Number of ways in which 10 countries can form into x alliances

Number of alliances (x)	Alliance structure	Alliance pattern
1	1	1
2	5	511
3	8	9,330
4	9	34,105
5	7	42,525
6	5	22,827
7	3	5,880
8	2	750
9	1	45
10	1	1
Total	42	115,975

A final variant of the problem is a division of the nations into five categories. Again there are two antagonistic powers, A and J, who form the core of two alliances respectively. We have another category of 'true neutrals', consisting of at least one country. If suitable inducements were offered, they might be willing to go in with either side. Italy, in the period before and during the early part of the first world war, was in this sort of position. We then have two further categories of 'biased neutrals', each again with at least one member. The first group of biased neutrals might stay neutral or they might go into alliance with A. They would not, however, consider going in with J—India might be in this situation today. The other group consists of nations who might consider going in with J but not with A. Assuming that there must always be one representative of each type of neutral, but that either A or J or both can be alone, then there are 18 possible different alliance structures and 5,418 different alliance patterns.

Some of the salient features of this sort of problem can be summarised in the table on page 89 of the different possible alliance patterns and structures which can be formed from a system of ten nations. The formidable number of possibilities is very apparent. Further, the number of nations involved is still very small. The possibilities are vastly magnified if the numbers of nations involved increases by very much.

The purpose of a theory of alliances is to provide some principles by which we can specify what particular alliance structures and patterns will grow up, and the conditions under which one pattern will develop into another. The purpose of the theory is to cut down the enormous number of possibilities to a much narrower range. This, in a sense, is what all theories are for, but the range of possibilities in this particular problem is unusually large.

2 The Theory of Alliance Growth

An alliance forms because it is in the interests of all the members that it should do so. Normally, at least, they would derive benefits from membership of the alliance denied to them if they were to act independently. However, they will get different advantages from being allied with different powers, and from alliances of different size[29].

First we shall discuss a simple problem involving the size of alliances, and then examine an equally simplified question involving a nation which might join one of two different alliances.

There is a superficial presumption that an alliance, particularly for warlike purposes, will grow as large as possible because the larger an alliance is, the more powerful it will seem. This might also seem to be the case with peaceful alliances such as customs unions, though, as the attitudes of France within the European Economic Community seem to have indicated, it is certainly not always seen that way. However, even with armed alliances, the presumption that an alliance will benefit by growing as large as possible has some weaknesses. To have a new member of an alliance has drawbacks as well as advantages, so the existing members will accept a supplicant's application only if it appears that his contribution to the alliance will outweigh any drawbacks involved.

This seems a fairly trivial proposition and not one which anyone is likely to dispute seriously. However, it does have some implications which, though fairly obvious when brought out into the open, can easily be overlooked. Suppose that the alliance is a military one. While the new member will presumably agree to using some of its armed forces to further the aims of the alliance, it also provides extra territory which the alliance has to defend. Whether or not there is a net benefit depends on the particular situation. There are further complications in integrating the various military plans of the allies if, for instance, there are linguistic differences between the supplicant and the other alliance members. The disruption of the military organisation involved in accommodating a new member might well outweigh the benefits of his participation. Again, a new member of an alliance is unlikely to have interests which are identical with those of all the other members, and they might therefore find themselves unwillingly involved in, and embarrassed by, some escapade entered into by the new member. The risk of this might well cause them to look with a jaundiced eye at a new member if his international conduct is unduly ebullient. So, while a new member may bring added strength to an alliance, he will also bring added responsibilities, and it is by no means certain that the existing members of an alliance will welcome with open arms any new member just for the sake of a few extra divisions.

The obvious implication of this is that an alliance will not always strive to grow as large as it can. A big alliance is not necessarily the best alliance, even in situations when it is genuinely more powerful than a smaller one. It is possible for an alliance to diminish in overall power if it grows unwieldy. However, this is not the crucial point, as it would presumably be widely accepted that this is a possibility. The more interesting implication of the analysis is that an alliance will stop acquiring extra members at some point before it has reached its potentially most powerful state. The alliance, qua alliance, could get stronger. However, each individual member would get weaker if the benefits of increased power were outweighed by the costs of achieving it in terms of adding new members.

This can be illustrated diagramatically (see Fig. 6.1, p. 92).

We place the various countries along the horizontal axis in order of their net contribution to the alliance—that which makes the greatest contribution being at the left hand end. For convenience, we also assume that this is the order of their joining the alliance. The gross value of the alliance to all powers added together is represented by the line marked 'benefit', and the costs to the alliance are represented by the line marked 'cost'. The vertical dotted lines represent the net total value of the alliance (in military terms this might be thought of as power). Now the alliance is at its strongest when G is included as a member, leaving H excluded. However, the benefit to the existing members of the alliance is at its greatest if E, F and G are also excluded, as the drawbacks of their allegiance are greater than their contribution. If A and B were the original members of the alliance, they would be well advised to

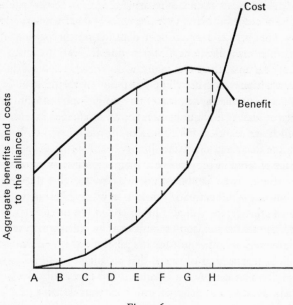

Figure 6.1

invite C and D to join them, but unwise to invite the others. Whether international politics is conducted on such a rational basis is, however, open to
doubt, but it is a helpful first approximation.

Qualifications and elaborations of such a simple theory are numerous.
However, it is intended as a prolegomena rather than a serious theory in its
own right. One obvious qualification is to the implied assumption of the
model that, if the new member of an alliance adds to the over-all value of that
alliance, the benefits of his association will be felt by all the members. If some
feel harmed by his inclusion and there is no way of securing any compensation from the benefiting powers, then a new range of problems is produced.
This raises the question of how to distribute the benefits which the new
member has added amongst the whole membership of the alliance, which puts
us back into the sort of bargaining problem discussed in chapter 5.

Whether the new member joins or not also depends to some extent on the
agreements made at the initial formation of the alliance to cope with such
problems (and such agreements are normally made). The agreement could be
to abide by a majority decision, but it is more likely that each member has a
veto. Alternatively there may be some special form of majority required such
as one which weighs countries according to their importance, needs a two-

thirds majority or specifies that almost any of the multifarious voting systems which can be imagined must be used. How far countries would abide by such agreements when made is, in any case, problematic. Except when a large power coerces a small one (which is not unheard of), it is hard to prevent a country leaving an alliance if it really wishes to do so.

In an international system where there are rival alliances, the opposing sides often try to persuade the neutral powers to join them or, if there is no hope of this, at least to remain neutral. Again using a simplified theory, we shall discuss the problems of 'Wooing the Neutral'.

Suppose the dominant members of two separate alliances both wish for the allegiance of some neutral power which, in the terminology of the first section, is a true neutral. On the whole, the neutral would prefer to remain that way, but might be persuaded to join either of the alliances if sufficient inducement were offered. Further, he has no preferences for either alliance and will go for the highest bidder. This seems a trivial problem—simply of deciding which side will bid the highest—but it has ramifications, and we wish to discuss two separate possibilities. The first is where the two opposing alliances are not on speaking terms, and only make deals with each other with difficulty. The second is where there is a reasonably high level of communication between the two sides—a situation, in other words, where effective negotiation can take place.

Let us pose the problem in stylised terms, which imply a measurement of the national interest. This assumption can be dropped (in form, but not substance) only at the expense of additional complexity in the argument. The countries concerned are Paflagonia and Crim Tartary who are rivals, and Neutralis which is neutral in their quarrel [30]. Neutralis is willing to forgo the advantages of a neutral status if it gets benefits from the alliance of 10 national interest units. These benefits might be in the form of foreign aid, defence commitments or indeed anything worth that amount to Neutralis. Crim Tartary is willing to pay, in some terms valued by Neutralis, a total of 15 national interest units. This figure is derived partly from the direct value of Neutralis' friendship and partly because of the drawbacks to Crim Tartary if Neutralis were affiliated to Paflagonia. In a similar way, Paflagonia would be willing to forgo 30 national interest units for an agreement with Neutralis. Which alliance does Neutralis enter, and on what terms? We shall assume for the moment that it does enter one of the alliances, and leave the possibility that it remains neutral for a little later.

Now we can pose this problem as a three person, zero sum game, or, more properly, a constant sum game (which may, at first sight, look surprising). Let us call the size of the 'payment' made by whoever is successful, B (for bribe). If Paflagonia makes this payment, then we denote it by B_p, and if Crim Tartary makes it then it is B_c. Assuming that the government of Neutralis is reasonably astute, then it will take advantage of the coolness between Paflagonia and Crim Tartary to play them off against each other, conducting what could substantially be called an auction. Crim Tartary will withdraw from this when the 'price' has reached 15. How far beyond this Neutralis can induce Paflagonia to go would depend on their relative bargaining skills, but, if we assume a reasonable degree of knowledge and sophistication on the part of all parties, then presumably not very far. Let us assume that the bribe ends up by being 18. Now, the benefit to Paflagonia is the difference between the highest price it would have paid (30 units) and the actual price, namely $30 - 18 = 12$; and the benefit to Neutralis is the difference between the minimum price he would have accepted and the actual price, namely 8. Crim Tartary gets nothing. The total payoff of the three countries adds up to 20. It is obvious that this is a constant sum situation, for Crim Tartary will always get nothing and the other two countries will share out the difference between 30 and 10, namely 20 units. Thus, although Neutralis is guaranteed at least 5 units, because Crim Tartary would be ready to pay that amount, eventually Paflagonia will always be able to attract Neutralis to its side for a total bribe of somewhere in between 15 and 30.

Now let us assume that Paflagonia and Crim Tartary are willing to make bargains with each other. Crim Tartary might agree not to bid up the price which Paflagonia pays to Neutralis in consideration of a payment from Paflagonia to itself of, let us say, 3 national interest units. This could come in the form of a concession by Paflagonia, enabling some other dispute to be settled in Crim Tartary's favour. Suppose that Paflagonia now pays the three units to Crim Tartary and a further 11 units to Neutralis—which is still worth while from the Neutralis point of view. The total benefits of the whole operation would then be 1 for Neutralis, 3 for Crim Tartary and 16 for Paflagonia. This adds up to 20 benefit units, and it is fairly easy to see that the total gain from any other arrangement of this sort would also be 20 units. Paflagonia and Crim Tartary would both have benefited at the expense of Neutralis and there would have been very little Neutralis could have done about it.

The pattern of alliance would be the same in this case as in the earlier one— Neutralis would go in with Paflagonia—but the bribes would be substantially different. One significant aspect of this is that the form of the bribe offered to Crim Tartary might involve concessions in some other conflict, so the behaviour in this bargain can have some effect on the rest of the system. This could not have been the case in the simple auction situation.

This model can be illustrated in diagrammatic terms. There is an interesting geometrical theorem which states that, in an equilateral triangle, the sum of the perpendicular distances from any point in it to the three sides is the same, no matter which point is selected; also, that this sum equals the perpendicular height of the triangle.

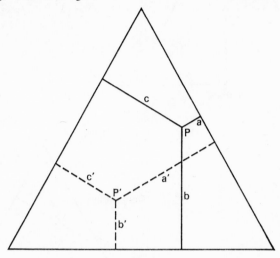

Figure 6.2

Thus $a + b + c = a' + b' + c'$ no matter which points P and P' are taken. To illustrate the theory, consider Figure 6.3 (a), which is an equilateral triangle with a height of 20 units which is the quantity to be divided up. Take a point Q in this triangle. The pay-off to Neutralis is represented by n, the pay-off to Paflagonia by p and the pay-off to Crim Tartary by c. The total of these is 20.

Let us take the initial situation, where Crim Tartary and Paflagonia had an 'auction' which Paflagonia won. Crim Tartary's 'profit' was zero, Paflagonia's was 12 and Neutralis' was 8. This is represented by the point A on Figure 6.3 (b). Neutralis would not accept from Paflagonia a bribe of less than 5, represented by point F, for he could get as much by approaching Crim Tartary. The general solution of this auction must therefore be represented by a point somewhere on the line FN.

Now let us consider the alliance model. First let us find the point where Neutralis has a profit of 1, Crim Tartary of 3 and Paflagonia of 16. This is represented by point B in Figure 6.3 (c), which is within the little triangle FPK —an area of some significance. The line FK, which is parallel with NC and

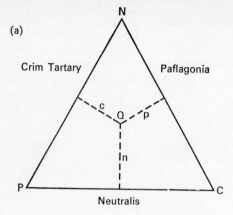

(a)

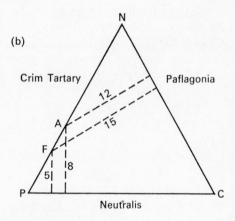

(b)

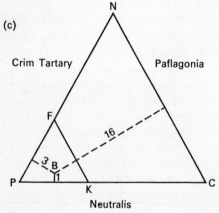

(c)

Figure 6.3

96

15 units away from it, represents all the different combinations of pay-offs for Crim Tartary and Neutralis which are consistent with Paflagonia getting 15 units. Now 15 units (or just under) are what Paflagonia could get in the auction arrangement. Paflagonia can always force an auction by refusing an agreement with Crim Tartary, and as neither Crim Tartary nor Neutralis can offer the other sufficient inducement to defect from this course, then Paflagonia will enter into no bargain which would result in a gain of less than 15 units. Hence, if any bargain is struck between Paflagonia and Crim Tartary, it will lie somewhere to the left of FK, that is, within the triangle FPK. Clearly, Paflagonia and Crim Tartary should now try to squeeze Neutralis as much as possible, driving the latter's gain down to 10 units (i.e. onto the line PC) and then share the proceeds. The only problem is how to divide them. It will be noticed now that, as far as Crim Tartary and Paflagonia are concerned, they are in the sort of bargaining situation discussed in Chapter 6, FPK being the bargaining set and PK being the boundary which they would both like to reach. If they were to adopt Nash's rule in order to achieve an agreement, then they would select a point half way between P and K. This would be called a 'fair swindle', at least by Neutralis.

The precise point at which the bargain is settled in the triangle FPK is not determined by the theory, a further extension (possibly of the theory in Chapter 5, Section 3) being required if we are to say any more about it. We could even leave the problem to be determined within the residual 'Don't Know' category of 'Bargaining Skill'.

It has so far been assumed that some alliance would form, the problem having been to decide which one (this has turned out to be the same irrespective of whether or not there is communication between Crim Tartary and Paflagonia), and on what terms such an alliance would be made (which are rather different with and without communication). What are the conditions under which no alliance will form? At first sight it would seem that an alliance would always be formed, as the benefits to both Crim Tartary and Paflagonia would always be greater than the drawbacks to Neutralis. This superficial result is due to the fact that we combined two factors—the positive desirability of the alliance as advancing the countries' interests, and the negative desirability which came from stopping the other country forming the alliance. Suppose that, in the case of Paflagonia, the positive desirability is represented by 5 units and the value of the alliance as a means of stopping Crim Tartary is 25 units; in the case of Crim Tartary, the two numbers are 8 and 7 respectively. In this case, neither Paflagonia nor Crim Tartary would want to form the alliance because of its positive attraction, as the 'price' either is willing to pay to Neutralis is less than the price Neutralis would demand.

Assuming that both know this, then neither will fear the other, and the negative attractions will be irrelevant to the issue. However, if both the positive and negative values of the alliance to Paflagonia were to be 15, it would be worth Paflagonia's making a bid for Neutralis' allegiance irrespective of Crim Tartary's attitude. However, this then activates the benefit to Crim Tartary of keeping Paflagonia out (or, as it happens, of being able at least to derive some compensation when the alliance goes through), and the process we have been discussing gets going.

This theory, like the others, is simple, but it does give some impression of the mechanics of the problem. One obvious simplification is the assumption that, if one country does something which costs one national interest unit and which benefits another country, the other country will gain by the same amount. This is how we get the constant sum restriction. However, this is a legitimate simplification in order to get at the basic elements of the problem, and serves the same sort of purpose as the cavalier assumption about the existence of a measure of national interest. The virtue of this sort of theory is as a clarifying device which might lead, at some stage, to a more sophisticated theory of coalition formation with wider applicability to the behaviour of the real world.

3 The Statistical Theory of Alliances

Like so much else in the theory of conflict behaviour, the theory of alliances consists of an unintegrated mixture. The theories which are formulated are not always the theories tested, and the generalisations tested are based more on plausible intuitions than on a sound body of deductive theory. However, as we have argued earlier, the process of the fusion of theory and testing is the process of scientific advance, and the relationships which are discussed in this chapter provide a statistical picture of the international system, which is a prerequisite of a more integrated body of theory.

Two separate questions will be discussed. First, some interesting results which have been obtained about the size of alliances in war (a restricted, but important aspect of the theory of alliances) and, secondly, some results on the relationship between the formation of alliances and the onset of war.

The basic data on the number of nations fighting on each side in various wars are given on page 99.

This shows, for instance, that there were 2 wars between an alliance of three members and one of two members. Also, of the 91 wars reported here, 42 were between single nations on both sides and therefore did not involve alliances except in the limiting sense. This is perhaps a larger proportion than might have been expected.

The Theory of Alliances

Number of Nations on either side in wars

Size: Greater than Magnitude 3·5. Period: 1820–1939

Number of nations	1	2	3	4	5	6	7	8	9
1	42	24	5	5	2	1	2	0	1
2		3	2	1	1	0	0	0	0
3			0	1	0	0	0	0	0

There was also 1 war of 15 vs. 5.   Source: Richardson

In chapter 3, section 3, we discussed some of the principles involved in the formulation and testing of statistical hypotheses. It is possible to calculate the theoretical distributions of various attributes if certain random processes are assumed, and to compare these results with the actual events in question. If actual and theoretical distributions coincide sufficiently closely, then this is evidence in favour of the random process posited to derive the theoretical distribution, being that which is operative in the real world.

The argument starts off, not with states, but with groups of individual people [31]. The distribution of the size of groups formed for warlike purposes such as bandit gangs, is markedly different from that of those formed for peaceful purposes such as at a cocktail party. The difference in size distribution seems to indicate a contrast between the way new members enter the group or leave it, or both.

Suppose one looks at the number of people talking together at a cocktail party. At any given time, there will be a number of groups of two, a number of groups of three, and a smaller number of larger groups such as six. There will also be a number of people standing on their own, in transition between groups and so on. These are the isolates or the 'groups' with only one member. If we take a number of snapshot counts of the groups in the party, counting on each occasion the number of groups of any given size, and if we tabulate our results, we will get a distribution in the same way as described in chapter four. We would then be able to see what probabilistic process generates a similar distribution of group sizes.

Now, clearly, the size of a group is determined by the rate of entry into and exit from the group. We are not attempting to discover why one particular group is bigger than another particular group, or why Sally joined the group which had Peter in it; we just want to obtain some general principle which governs entry into and exit from groups. As these rules are probabilistic, we get different groups of different sizes. Furthermore, any theoretical distribution is unlikely to fit perfectly. Now a theoretical distribution which is relevant must be deduced from particular probabilistic rules of entry and exit. One such rule is that entry into a group is independent of its size, while the rate at which people leave is proportional to the size. Put slightly differently, this means that people join groups without taking any particular notice of how big the group is, being as ready to talk with just one other person as with a group of five. Similarly, they stay as long with a small group as with a large one. So, because more people are in it, a group of six is more likely to lose a member in any given five minutes than is a group of two. This is intuitively plausible in a context such as a cocktail party though, of course, it is by no means the only possible intuitively appealing set of rules. This particular case gives what is called a *truncated Poisson* distribution of group sizes. This is the Poisson distribution (see Chapter 4) with no zero values as, in the present context, the notion of a group of zero size is meaningless.

In an empirical study of various groups which formed at swimming pools, in play groups, in the street, and so on (but not actually at cocktail parties, though the groups might be expected to have similar characteristics), the group sizes followed the truncated Poisson distribution very closely, which is evidence in favour of the entry and exit rules posited being the correct ones.

The groups examined were all formed for peaceful purposes. There are also two studies of warlike groups of individuals collected by Richardson. The first consists of the statistics of the size of bandit gangs in Manchuokuo (not directly measured but plausibly inferred), and the second is of the size of Chicago gangs in the nineteen twenties. These two studies show that the size distributions of two very different groups are remarkably similar, but are clearly dissimilar from the size distributions of groups formed for peaceful purposes. The warlike case approximates to the Yule distribution, which can be derived by assuming that new entrants to an alliance come in at a rate proportional to the size of the existing alliance, while, once in, members do not leave (or very rarely). Exit only occurs when the group disintegrates and all the members simultaneously revert to the status of isolates.

These observations are suggestive, but no more. They acquire an added suggestive significance when we look at the distribution of nations in war coalitions. Using the table on page 99 as a basis, we can derive the number of alliances of particular sizes which fought wars during the period 1820 to 1939. Thus there were a total of 34 occasions when alliances of two members fought—24 when an alliance of 2 fought an alliance of one, 3 when a pair of alliances of two fought each other, 2 occasions when two countries fought three and 1 each of two fighting four and two fighting five.

The figures for the theoretical Yule distribution are given for comparison. It can be seen that they are sufficiently close to the actual ones for it to be plausible that the same probabilistic hypothesis explains the hypothetical and the actual data—that, for warlike purposes, the number of nations joining alliances is proportional to their size, and that alliances break up rather than lose members in the middle of their career. As this is a statistical hypothesis, it does not mean that alliances never lose members, only that it is comparatively unusual.

No. of nations in an alliance (x)	1	2	3	4	5	6	7	8 and more
No. of alliances of size x	124	34	8	7	4	1	2	2
Theoretical (Yule) distribution	128	29	11	5	3	2	1	2

These observations are a long way from providing a theory of alliances, even if they can be shown to be more generally applicable. They do, however, suggest some factors which should receive predominant consideration and rule out some possibilities as being implausible. For example, they are inconsistent with the pattern which would be generated if nations were attracted to smaller alliances, as might be implied by some versions of the balance of power theory.

The second and rather different statistical problem is that concerning the relationship between alliance formation and the occurrence of war[32]. Behind much of the traditional concern with alliances has been the notion of the balance of power. This has been a popular theoretical concept, though rarely precisely described. Indeed, it has not always been clear whether it is meant to be prescriptive for the international system or a description of certain aspects of it. However, it is clear that two things are involved in any discussion of it. First, it involves alliances or potential alliances and, in some sense, must be subsumed under a theory of alliances. Secondly, the pattern of alliances is relevant to the frequency of war—some alliance patterns (those pertaining when the system is in balance) making war less likely (or possibly less destructive), and other patterns making war more likely.

The investigations were based around the notion that the more alliance commitments there are in the international system, the less flexible it is and the more prone to war. The basic phenomenon to be measured, therefore, was the reduction of independent units in the international system. Two separate but related variables were used: alliance aggregation and the tendency of nations to form into two hostile camps (bipolarity). Both propositions were tested with a time lag (three years emerged as the best) as one would not expect any reaction to an alliance to be immediate.

In both cases, the results were markedly different in the nineteenth and the twentieth centuries. In the twentieth century there is a clear positive relationship between alliance aggregation and the onset of war, and between the degree of bipolarisation and the onset of war. However, in the nineteenth century the reverse result holds. These results hold, even if different measures of war and of alliance aggregation are used, and do not appear to be artefacts of the particular indices.

The empirical evidence is rather hard to interpret in the framework of alliance theories, whether ancient or modern, but, as it is hard to interpret in any framework, what we have is a phenomenon in search of a theory. Until the phenomenon is explained by more than casual suggestions, we are deceiving ourselves if we think we have a theory of alliances.

The results are clear but surprising. However, as one of the functions of a statistical test of informal theoretical notions is to discover the unexpected as well as the expected result, the study is important. We are left without any adequate explanation of the relationship between alliance formation and war, which represents a major challenge for further theorisation.

chapter seven

International Crises

1 The Nature of an International Crisis

Among the more noticeable types of event are the crises which intermittently erupt between nations. From time to time, the politically conscious sections of the public nervously snatch at their newspapers to see whether impending doom has approached closer or receded. By its nature, the international crisis represents some deviation from the normal pattern of international behaviour. It is nevertheless a particularly important type of event, for it is often these periods of international trauma that trigger off war, and from which new patterns of behaviour emerge or are consolidated. The fact that a period of crisis is abnormal does not diminish its importance, for its effects are great. A period of physical illness in a human being is abnormal, but for similar reasons it is a very important area of study.

In order to develop a theory of crises, it is necessary first to have some definition of the event. A period of crisis has many characteristics but, initially, we shall postulate one or two of these as defining characteristics, as against those which are observed to accompany such situations. In another terminology, we shall start by defining the necessary, as opposed to the contingent, characteristics of a crisis situation.

The first stage in a practical problem of definition is to ask what particular events should be covered by it. Clear cases of international crises in general terminology are the Cuba Missiles crisis of 1962, the crisis over Berlin in 1948, the Munich crisis, the crisis of the summer of 1914, and the multitude of crises among the various European powers in the two decades before the first world war. Other possibilities could be included, but, for the moment, we shall concern ourselves with a definition which encompasses these.

The simplest definition which covers them all involves two factors. First, a crisis situation is one of great uncertainty, where the possibility of a really disastrous conclusion to the crisis is quite large. In the words of an earlier section, the gap in utility between the best and worst likely solutions is very great as compared to that between the best and worst solutions of any normal uncertain situation. The second defining characteristic is that the crisis involves an abnormal degree of pressure on the decision makers in that it is carried on over a relatively short period of time. Both these characteristics must be examined in greater detail.

The first feature of a crisis is a general characteristic involved in other contexts than the international. A crisis in medicine, such as that which frequently occurred in pneumonia prior to the development of anti-biotics, was a period of doubt where the patient could die—which is typically regarded as disastrous—or recover, essentially restoring the *status quo ante*. The utility interval—if the term is appropriate—between these two extreme alternatives is very wide, particularly for the patient. Similarly, in international crises there is a short period in which the chances of war breaking out become really significant (a conclusion which only a few would regard as anything but very unfortunate). The alternative, much preferred is a peaceful resolution to the crisis, either by a compromise or a return to the *status quo*. In both the medical and the international example, a significant possibility of disaster is abnormal. The usual state in both cases is one where there is only a small probability of disaster in the near future from unexpected causes (a heart attack or a sudden invasion by a neighbour), but where there is a constant significant possibility that some situation will become a little disadvantageous (the patient or potential patient may catch a cold, or the country may suffer some diplomatic reverse). Normalcy involves moderate chances of small reverses and small chances of large reverses. A crisis, however, involves high chances of large reverses, which is what makes it so disturbing.

The second defining feature we claimed for a crisis is that it takes place over a relatively short period of time—a few days or weeks in the case of international crises of the type we are considering. In this period, the rate at which decisions have to be made and information circulated, both within the foreign offices and between foreign offices, is much greater than is normal. This speed of operation has a number of consequences, such as that the full decision-making and consultative process cannot always be gone through properly, a more superficial and rapid selection and inspection of the documentation taking place, and that the individuals involved in the decision-making process are put under severe mental and physical pressures which may distort their judgements. These, then, are added features of the crisis situation which we must examine, but notice that they are consequences of, rather than the defining features themselves. Thus there are situations other than international crises where a decision-maker is placed under abnormal stress, so it would be inappropriate to define an international crisis as one where the individuals are under stress.

The defining characteristics which we have suggested exclude a number of situations which are sometimes referred to as crisis situations. Thus the Viet

Nam war has been referred to as the Viet Nam crisis despite the fact that it is not a short-lived affair. A perfectly acceptable definition of crisis would contain just the first of our criteria, but would have the drawback that there are many features of the acute crisis which are not present in the longer period affair—such as inadequate selection of information on which to base judgements. It is thus convenient to distinguish between the two categories, as they have substantially different characteristics.

A crisis does seem to be a very appropriate feature of the international system for analysis by the methods of the social scientists, which no doubt accounts for the considerable interest which has been displayed in these events. It fits most appropriately into the rubric of Karl Popper's definition of the task of the social scientist as being 'to trace the unintended social repercussions of international human actions'[33]. The features which make it appropriate are that it is a relatively limited and clear-cut phenomenon. It may be that chance elements play a significant part in the determination of the course of a crisis, but it should be possible to identify when these chance elements are significant. This being so, the aim of the social scientist in this field—to produce a workable theory of crisis behaviour—would seem to be attainable, conceivably in the not-too-distant future.

Such a theory should be able to identify what features of a crisis lead it to develop one way rather than another—into a war rather than a restoration of the *status quo*. The propositions should have general applicability to most, if not all, crises, and the theory's idealised crisis would not be a perfect picture of any particular event, but would contain some elements common to all crises. In this way it is like the theory of trade cycles, which describes no trade cycle which has ever taken place but which has sufficient in common with all (or most) real trade cycles to make the theory a meaningful description of the salient aspects of the real phenomena.

The attractions of a theory of crises extend beyond those of satisfying intellectual curiosity. If a satisfactory theory can be formulated and appropriately tested, then it might be possible to make recommendations on how to behave in an international crisis so as not to involve the world in disaster. Clearly statesmen have some crude notions of how crises develop—as Kennedy and Khruschev obviously did in the Cuba Missiles Crisis. However, a theory of crises would be a much firmer basis and would increase the likelihood of a peaceful resolution of such situations.

2 Interacting Decisions

A crisis centres around the decisions and actions taken by two or more national decision-making groups, where the actions of one are an important, and perhaps the predominant, determinant of the responses of the others.

In any sort of social situation, the actions of one social unit, whether it be an individual or a group, affect the others, and to some extent provide a stimulus for their actions. At a crude level a social situation can therefore be described as a sequence of actions in which one party's behaviour provides a stimulus to another, causing it to respond which, in turn, provides a stimulus to the initiating party. Descriptions of social situations using this naïve 'input-output' model as a basis could not be expected to get very far. However, it is useful as a starting point.

The relations between nations are also social situations in the sense that the actions of one affect the decisions and hence actions of another, the social units involved being the national decision-making groups which can loosely but conveniently be called 'the governments'. In crisis situations, the interactions become much more intense than in normal times and it is the resulting abnormalities which it is the function of a theory of crises to examine.

We can look at two sorts of abnormalities. First, there is the alteration in the decision-making process itself. As a result of the increased pressure caused by the quicker flow of information and the need for more rapid decision, a number of stages get by-passed and altered. Secondly, the perceptions of the decision makers alter as the tension in a crisis increases. They tend to see the world in increasingly stark black-and-white terms as the tension increases. The two factors interact, of course: the change in the decision-making process is, in part, a consequence of the altered structure of perceptions. However, it is convenient to separate the two, and we shall discuss the effects on the process in section 3 and on perceptions in section 5. Both, and in particular the alteration in the process, will be described in terms of normality. The normal decision-making process with which the problem of deviance can be compared is discussed towards the end of this section.

It will simplify the problem and not detract too much from realism to consider a crisis involving only two countries. These are by no means unknown—the Cuba Missiles crisis essentially involved just two participants, Cuba itself being barely considered as a decision-making body, while other countries like the United Kingdom which tried hopefully to appear important, failed abysmally. In examining the two-party crisis, we shall be able to see many of the essential principles which operate in crisis situations. In this section we shall discuss a general picture of the decision-making process which applies to any situation of interacting decisions, and then from this base discuss the peculiarities of the crisis situation.

The simplest model of an interacting decision system is the stimulus-response model mentioned above. This is represented in the diagram below and, as is clear, it is practically devoid of content.

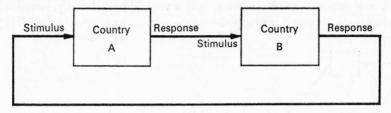

Figure 7.1

The value of such a model lies only in its schematic representation of a process. This is an extreme case of a 'black box' theory where there is no enquiry into what goes on inside the black box. If certain stimuli always provoked the same responses, then a theory involving only these black box categorisations would be adequate for the formulation of a theory of crises. However, this is not the case, so it is necessary to provide a somewhat richer framework.

A slightly less basic model of crisis behaviour involves the perceptions which the various states have of each other, and the actions they take on the basis of these perceptions. It is clear that in any situation, an act acquires importance (if it acquires any) because of the way in which it is perceived by the person against whom it is directed. There is no particular reason why the object of some act or statement should attribute the same degree of importance to it as the actor. A characteristic of a stable social situation is that the participants more or less agree as to the significance of particular acts. If this is not so, then the situation is likely to be unstable in that inappropriate responses to various acts will occur. This is, in fact, one of the features of a crisis situation. The participants' perceptions of the situation differ, commonly by assuming others to be more hostile than they see themselves, so an unstable situation can rapidly be made worse. This is discussed in greater detail in the final section of this chapter.

A decision taken in response to altered circumstances can be simplified to involve four processes. Firstly, there is the reception of information in the form of raw data; secondly this information is processed and evaluated, i.e. the important is sifted from the unimportant and the implications of various pieces of information are assessed; thirdly, the information is passed on to the decision makers who decide what to do; and finally, if any action is to be taken, the agency involved (the army, for example) has to be instructed and the decision carried out. In practice, these stages are not as distinct as is implied here and are frequently intertwined. On the other hand, the decision process could be split into much smaller stages. This formulation, however, is useful for our purposes even if it is necessarily a very, almost absurdly, simplified scheme; it is illustrated below. (Fuller representations are given in [34] and [35].)

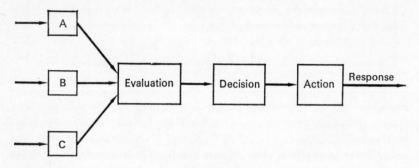

Figure 7.2

Information is received by the government from a variety of different sources represented by boxes A, B and C. The information might be about the actions of some other state or, alternatively, be a message received from that state. So box A could represent the passage of official diplomatic messages via the embassy in another country, or, in more strained times, communicated directly between the two governments. Box B could also represent communications from the embassy in the other country, but would consist of the evaluations of the situation by the ambassador. Box C could represent intelligence reports. There are clearly other sources of information, such as newspapers (whether these are officially primed with information or unofficial organs), official statements not directly expressed in the form of communications, and so on. Information comes into the country from one or more of these sources and they are not always in agreement—intelligence reports and ambassadors' evaluations can, and frequently do, contradict each other.

These raw data are then passed on to the government, which normally means the Foreign Office or sometimes the Defence Department. The function of the Foreign Office is to process information, evaluate it, and, when necessary, pass it on in a suitable form for decision by the Minister. Although in principle, this stage is one of processing and evaluation, it is difficult to separate it from a decision-making stage as minor decisions (judged by fairly high standards) have to be taken by the bureaucracy to avoid overwhelming the necessarily small group of top decision-makers. In the case of larger issues, the decision-maker is still very much in the hands of his advisers, because they are the people who sift and condense information so that it is possible, in a short time, to comprehend the issues. But the digesting of information necessarily distorts it to some extent, no matter how conscientious and impartial the official might be. In any case, Foreign Office officials are asked their opinions on various aspects of policy, which therefore ensures some participation in the decision process.

The decision itself may be taken by a variety of people. A great deal of foreign policy is decided by a Head of State along with his Foreign Secretary. The relative importance of the two can vary widely. For instance, when Eisenhower was President of the United States, Dulles was clearly the prime foreign policy decision-maker. Kennedy, however, effectively ran his own foreign policy, at least in its most important aspects. Cabinet approval may be required for some things and, in the case of treaties and major long-term agreements, the approval of the legislature is required in countries where the latter's agreement is not fore-ordained. Who takes the decision depends to a large extent on what the decision is. However, as far as decisions taken in crises are concerned, the group of people involved is quite small.

A decision is the selection of a course of action—which may be to do nothing at all. It may also be to send a message of some sort, and the bulk of Foreign Office decisions are naturally of this character. In this case, the activity remains within 'the Government' but, when physical action such as some military move, is being taken, then the appropriate people must be informed and instructed. The distinction between decision and action becomes significant.

What the government finally does or says becomes the input for another government, and a similar process is enacted.

The decision making structures of different countries are not, of course, all the same. However, the processes described must operate in some form or other, and agencies must be set up to deal with them. Information must be acquired, processed, decided and then acted upon, so perhaps it is not surprising that the administrative structures which states have evolved to cope with these problems are not too dissimilar.

3 The Decision Process in Crises

A crisis has been defined as a situation where the outcome is seen as potentially disastrous. The decisions which have to be taken are thus regarded as important by the decision makers and, partly as a consequence of this, there is a much greater flow of information through the system than is normally the case. In down to earth terms, this simply means that more people send more memoranda, diplomatic communications and so forth. This is true both between the countries involved and within the countries. The increased message flow, coupled with the unusually large number and the importance of many of the decisions to be made, are characteristics of crisis decision making, and the system obviously has, in some way, to adjust to this unusual circumstance.

The way in which officials cope with the increased information is, typically, by not coping with it at all—the system suffers an 'information overload'. Data is not processed at all, and reports go unread or, when they are, are not assimilated into the consciousness of the relevant decision-maker in such a way that they are appropriately allowed for in making the decision.

The crux of the process is clearly at the decision-making stage itself, rather than at the information receival and processing stages, and we can examine the system starting at this point. The decision-making stage acts in a way which, at first sight, seems paradoxical, given the increased flow of message information and the increased number of decisions which have to be taken. First, the decision-making group is reduced in size despite the fact that, in a sense, it has more to do; secondly, the decision-takers react more quickly to the actions of the rival than in non-crisis times, again despite the fact that there is more work to be done. The non-crisis reaction of a bureaucracy is, of course, to take longer in reaching a decision when subject to overload, rather than to move more rapidly. However, both these characteristics are only superficially surprising. The speed of reaction arises simply from the fact that the decisions are seen as so important as to need urgent action. The quick reaction is made possible by the necessarily extremely selective way in which the decision-takers consider the information. They compensate for having to deal with a larger volume of information simply by using a smaller proportion of it. The part they do consider, they act on very quickly because of the perception (sometimes correct) that if they do not do so, then some disastrous result will ensue (the disastrous result sometimes occurs in any case).

The shrinking of the decision-making group, usually to about five or six in number, also makes rapid decision-taking easier. A group this size can easily meet together and, if it is selected so that the members are in general agreement, it becomes relatively easy to reach decisions quickly. A larger group makes the process of discussion more complex. Further, as the effective decision-makers are not always physically close, some communication must be written, and the number of messages necessarily goes up very rapidly with the number of people involved. The shrinking, then, is a response to the pressure for speed in decision-taking, itself a consequence of the perceived importance of the problem in hand. In a sense it is also a direct way of coping with the problem of information overload. A group of people taking a decision are not dealing only with the information which comes from the outside to their group, but also with the different views of people within the group, which is a form of internally generated information. However, the less people are involved in the group, the less information of this sort there is to consider. Consequently, though superficially surprising, these characteristics of the crisis situation are less so when subjected to examination.

The tendency to quicker response and smaller decision-making groups appears to be true of all crises which have been studied, with the significant counter example of the Cuba missiles crisis[14, 15]. Here the opposite occurred, at least on the American side. The decision-making group was quite deliberately enlarged by President Kennedy in order to promote discussion, in the hope that a wider selection of alternatives would appear. Further, the group was explicitly allowed as much time as was possible for discussion, to avoid the dangers of immediate emotional reactions. The technique seems to have worked as a deliberate device for provoking relatively calm responses. We shall return to this case when discussing changing perceptions in times of crisis.

The problem of how decision-takers react to information overload still remains. Clearly they must be selective in the information considered. Part of the process of selection is accidental—the messages on top of the pile get dealt with more thoroughly than those at the bottom—but this is by no means the whole story. It must be remembered that the decision-takers are working very hard, probably getting inadequate sleep, and are involved in the stresses and tensions of taking very important decisions. Now, people under a great deal of stress do not act in the same way as in normal situations. Sometimes they improve their performance, but frequently, particularly when the stress is exaggerated by fatigue, their performance deteriorates—they become the victims of emotional preconceptions and are less able to evaluate the situation objectively. This affects information selection procedures. The decision-makers have to select information in some way, as they cannot hope to deal with everything. However, they tend to pay more attention to that information which confirms their earlier beliefs and prejudices and to deal cursorily with anything which contradicts the stereotypes they have of how the other country should be acting. Thus, they look for their information from sources which they know will confirm their earlier opinions. If the ambassador is sending reports which contradict the decision taker's preconceptions, while the intelligence service tends to confirm his prejudices, then the ambassador's reports will be filed and ignored and the intelligence service listened to eagerly. Given the stress which the decision-taker is under, this procedure is quite natural. He has to select information in some way, and this one at least cuts down what he has to consider. Further, when under stress he does not have the time, energy or inclination to try to rethink his world view, and the intellectually painful process of reconciling dissonant information with a firm, pre-existing viewpoint is most painlessly done by ignoring the information. The drawback is obviously that the decisions which result from this extremely biased selection of information are only accidentally the appropriate ones.

The characteristics of the decision-making process, viewed as a whole, are not very surprising. The last characteristic which we shall mention is also not unexpected, though perhaps less intimately connected with the rest. When a military action is contemplated, the decision-makers must give orders to the military leaders. However, it is not unusual for the military leaders to initiate the orders themselves and, in effect, to by-pass the proper decision-making apparatus. Two examples in the 1914 crisis were Churchill's keeping of the fleet on the alert despite not having been given the order to do so by the cabinet or Prime Minister, and the German Chief of Staff's mobilisation a day before he was ordered to do so. As it happened, neither of these moves had any serious escalatory effect, mainly because the escalation had already taken place, but either could have had very serious consequences. Thus, while the link between decision and action is fairly close, it is not perfect; also, within the action box there is a decision element which sometimes comes out, to the embarrassment of the Government.

This, then, is a picture of the decision process, viewed as a response to abnormal pressures, both on the system and the individuals who are members of it. What goes on within this altered system is to be discussed in section 5.

4 Crisis Behaviour: The Sources of Evidence

The number of events from which the generalised statements of the preceding section are derived are few, and the propositions must therefore not be treated with too great a respect. Further investigation might indicate that the patterns suggested are much less common than is currently supposed. However, a single counter instance would not refute the description of crisis behaviour. The possibility of counter examples will be magnified if a greater awareness by decision-makers of the mechanisms of crisis alters their behaviour, thus falsifying the theory. This would be an instance of a self-defeating prophecy. Self-consciousness about the 'normal' behaviour of decision makers in crises was, in fact, probably responsible for Kennedy's behaviour in the Cuba missiles crisis, which differed markedly from that of most statesmen in such situations.

Granted that only a few crises have been seriously investigated to date, and also that the total number of international crises is so limited that statistical significance as normally understood cannot be obtained, there still remains the problem of how the evidence is collected and the interpretation of what evidence there is.

As far as the actual decision processes are concerned, there are no severe methodological issues involved. By and large, it is possible, by using the normal sources of historical data, to find out who was talking or sending messages to whom, and who was involved in the making of various decisions. The record may not be perfect (particularly in the case of recent events, where the situation is frequently deliberately obscured for security and personal reasons) but, in general, it is quite adequate. The difficulties arise in finding out how perceptions change through the development of a crisis. The problem is not so much the lack of evidence, though this is a feature, but the interpretation of what evidence there is. On what basis, other than an intuitive one, does one say that the decision makers of one country perceived those of another in a more and more hostile light as some crisis proceeded? An intuitive assessment may not be wrong, but we want something more precise for serious analysis.

Two methods have been used, neither of which falls within the traditional canon of historical research. The first is Simulation and the second is Content Analysis[36]. As Simulation is dealt with in another chapter, we shall not discuss it further here.

Content Analysis is a technique by which written exchanges can be carefully evaluated, which, in some sense of the word, enables the measurement of perceptual variables such as 'hostility', 'friendship', 'tension' and so on, to be made. The idea of being able to measure such apparent intangibles as hostility might at first sight seem strange, though later in this section we shall argue that it involves far fewer methodological jumps than might appear to be the case.

First we shall describe, rather cursorily, the technique of Content Analysis, as it is applied to the study of the documentation of crisis situations. The records of spoken words are frequently missing, so the analysis is largely done on written documents, that is, the messages which were sent to and from the various decision makers and advisors, both within and between governments, at the time of a crisis. A document is first coded for analysis in the following way. Each statement made in the document is taken separately and regarded as an 'atomic theme'. Four attributes are associated with each of these units.

First, there is the perceiver of an act or state of affairs, that is, the person who makes the statement; secondly, there is the actor who is being perceived; thirdly, there is the person who is the object of the action involved; and finally, there is the nature of the act itself. This can be expressed diagrammatically, as in Figure 73. The perceiver in the top box sees everything in the large oblong below it. The perception consists of an actor, a target and a relationship between the two. For the questions in which we are interested, this can be thought of as a situation in which a subject has a transitive relationship with an object.

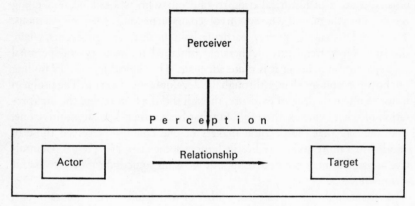

Figure 7.3

There need not be an entry in all categories. Thus a statement might not involve a target though, inasmuch as we are interested in one country's perception of another, this implies a target for all statements on that subject. It is also possible for the same entry to appear in two of the boxes. In particular, a country might have a perception of itself, either as an actor or as the target of an act or statement. However, a box may not have more than one entry. An atomic theme has only one subject and one object, so a sentence which has two objects, such as 'The British objected to the actions of Germany and Austria', is regarded as having two separate atomic themes, 'The British objected to the actions of Germany' and 'The British objected to the actions of Austria'. The number of expressions of a certain intention, feeling or descriptions of an action can therefore be counted, the critical part of the process being the definition of the atomic theme.

The next problem is the measurement of the intensity of the relationship expressed between the actor and the target. Perceptions are divided into various categories such as power, capability, friendship, and hostility. It is not immediately obvious how these variables are to be measured, and in what way such a measure, when constructed, is meaningful. We describe the method of measurement first, and then discuss its meaning.

The essential function of the measurement of the intensity of attitudes is to formalise the opinions of the observers. There are various techniques, in one of which a 'scaling judge' is given a large selection of statements, say on hostility, and asked to place each statement in one of nine different classes ranged from most to least intense. He is also obliged to get a certain proportion of the total statements into each category, the proportion in each class following the binomial distribution. That is, the percentage of statements which falls into each category must be as follows:

Category (Intensity rating)	1	2	3	4	5	6	7	8	9
Percentage in category	5	8	12	16	18	16	12	8	5

As one scaling judge alone leaves too much scope for individual idio-syncrasy, the scaling is done by several judges. If the conclusions of different judges were widely dissimilar, the method would be of dubious value but, in practice, agreement seems to be high. Related techniques are used to measure the intensity of actions, the relevant variable here being a violence—non-violence dimension.

Each statement which is relevant is thus categorised both according to the type of effect or action, and according to a measure of its intensity. A text can therefore be analysed, using these rules for measurement, and different texts can be compared for the degree of hostility, friendliness or whatever the characteristic under consideration might be, in a more formalised manner than would otherwise be possible.

The techniques of Content Analysis, and particularly the fitting of state-ments into the binomial distribution, looks to be arbitrary and unjustifiable. However, similar devices are widely used, for instance in the marking of examinations. This also involves evaluating pieces of work and putting them into various categories which are ranked from good to bad. These categories are given a number (the 'mark'), which, despite its arbitrary character, is then dealt with as if it were an ordinary number. Examination marking does not always involve forcing a percentage of examinees into a preconceived pattern —indeed, for small groups, this would be quite unjustifiable. However, it is common, when large numbers of students are examined, to assume that the marks will follow a distribution closely related to the binomial, and known as the *normal distribution*; and to look for an explanation if they do not do so.

To point out that the methodological techniques of Content Analysis are similar to those widely used in other fields is not not itself a justification of them. It may be that the other measures are also illegitimate. However, there is a firmer base from which to defend methods of the sort involved in Content Analysis.

Whenever there is an attempt to make some branch of knowledge more scientific, there is a move to make hitherto rather loosely expressed statements more precise. Further, the set of statements made concerning the subject matter has to be expressed in such a form that they can be tested. The tests to be applied must be such that they can be repeated by other investigators, so that there is wide acceptance that particular results confirm or refute the hypothesis. This usually means that concepts which previously have been rather loosely used must now be defined in a more rigorous way. This process has happened in physics, biology, economics and is now happening in the analysis of political behaviour. However, the more precise definitions may mean that the new concepts are slightly different from the old, and some degree of caution is needed in using the terms. The use of measures is one example of the redefinition process. The question is not so much 'Is hostility measurable?' as 'Is it possible to define hostility in a measurable manner?' In order to justify the continued use of the term hostility for a redefined concept there must be a relationship between the new and the old. Also, to justify the new definition within a newly developing scientific approach, the measured concept must lead to fruitful hypotheses. What is 'fruitful', however, is no longer a purely scientific judgement and ultimately depends on values.

There are, of course, many different ways of defining a concept such as hostility in a measurable way. The choice between them must be on the basis of their relative use in making fruitful predictions. There is nothing particularly revolutionary in this point of view. Frequently, in the natural sciences, there are measures which seem so natural that to fuss about with alternative definitions would be foolish. However, in the social sciences, the use of rather arbitrarily defined measures is widespread. Quantification is, in general, a pragmatic business which is justified by results, rather than by an appeal to the fundamental characteristics of things.

5 Perceptions and Actions in a Crisis

Comparing a crisis with a normal situation, there are differences not only in the decision procedures, but also in the types of decisions made. The way in which actions are perceived in such periods is rather different from normal, which is hardly surprising in view of the unusual pressure on the participants.

It is convenient, in discussing this problem, to employ a scheme differing slightly from that used earlier in the analysis of the decision process itself. We depict this in the diagram below [see also 36]:

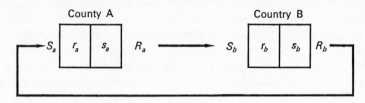

County A   Country B

$$S_a \quad r_a \quad s_a \quad R_a \longrightarrow S_b \quad r_b \quad s_b \quad R_b$$

Figure 7.4

The capital letters, S, denote the stimulus which a nation receives (for example, some form of military attack) and R are the physical responses which it makes to this act. The lower case letters, r, denote the perceptual response to the behaviour stimulus received, that is, the perception by the state of the attitudes and intentions of the rival state to itself, and s are the attitudes and intentions of the state towards its rival. If there were perfect perception, then s_a would equal r_b, and r_a would equal s_b. This perfect perception, or even reasonably good approximation to it, is just what is missing in a crisis situation.

The phenomenon of escalation is one which is widely found in crisis situations. This is simply a situation where one country behaves in a way which the other side perceives to be hostile. This evokes a hostile response, which the initiating party perceives as such—perhaps seeing it as more hostile than was intended—and it, in its turn, responds in a more hostile manner. If the process goes on long enough or gets out of hand, then the situation can lead into war. The whole process of escalation is still not very well understood. In the case of the 1914 crisis, for instance, which has been extensively investigated by a team at Stanford University led by Robert C. North, we can actually identify the points where the magnifying implicit in the escalation process took place. Further, there are various hypotheses about behaviour which would certainly lead to an escalation process in such tense situations (some of which we discuss later) that are confirmed both by intuition and fact. What is less clear is why de-escalation takes place in international crises, as, after all, it frequently does. Clearly, if we can offer insight into only one side of the phenomenon, without also being able to explain why it switches into another pattern on so many occasions, then the initial explanation is inadequate. However, some knowledge of the escalation process in particular crises exists, and, while it does not fit together completely, it is nevertheless reasonably coherent. A great deal of it is derived from examination of the 1914 crisis, so the earlier cautions concerning the degree of generality are still in order. However, while international crises are relatively infrequent in number, there is other information about how people and groups react to stress in other contexts, which is applicable to the crisis situation. Political decision-making groups are human groups, and general propositions about stress can be interpreted in that context.

In the 1914 crisis, one magnifying point appeared to be the S-r link in the case of the dual alliance (that is, Germany and Austria). Their conception of others' intentions towards them seems to have been consistently exaggerated; their response was to a rather higher level of stimulus than that to which they were really being exposed. This does not seem to have applied to the Triple Entente (Britain, France and Russia). Precisely why this should have occurred is not very clear, but at least the formulation has provided us with a technique for locating a source of strain.

The other consistently magnifying node, which this time applied to all the countries involved in the crisis, was the s-R point which represents the decision-action link in the earlier picture of the decision making process. Thus, the actual reactions in terms of military and other similar moves were consistently more violent than one would have been led to believe by the statements made about them. This is surprising. One expects countries to talk more boldly than they act, but, in this instance, the reverse is quite clearly the case. This, of course, also had a magnifying effect, as it is physical acts, rather than the verbal expressions, which stimulate reaction.

The extremely careful codification of the data which has been done by North and his team leaves little doubt that the 1914 crisis escalated in this way, or rather at these particular points. However, the explanations of the processes and how they differ from those of other crises in which, for instance, de-escalation occurred, are not yet known. All we have is a very elaborate case study, in which hitherto unmeasured variables are not merely quantified, but related to each other. The development of a theory adequate to explain, as distinct from describe, these phenomena is yet to come. It will require similar detailed studies of many other crises, and will have to explain their differences as well as their similarities.

There are other propositions, on the development of attitudes in crises, which are also predominantly based on the evidence of Content Analysis studies. There are obviously many possible ways of categorising these attitudes. One useful method is a classification into attitudes about the other parties to the crisis, and about the scope and nature of the actions which are available to the participant himself. In the first category comes the tendency to see the opponent in stereotyped terms—the Militaristic Prussian, Perfidious Albion, or, at a later date, atheistic communists and war-mongering, imperialistic capitalists. One of the characteristics of extreme images is that anything can be made to conform to the image in one way or another. This leads to another characteristic of the decision-maker's perceptions in such situations, which is the tendency to see any attempt at conciliation as either weakness or a trick, rather than taking it for what it might very well be, namely, a genuine attempt to reach an equitable settlement. If a person has an image of some group as being completely bad, and if the enemy then acts in a manner which would normally be interpreted as good, some less charitable explanation for it has to be found. Thus, the conciliatory act is interpreted as having been forced on one's opponent, or else as a deceitful subterfuge designed to mislead one into incautious trust. Third parties to the direct crisis are viewed more and more as being either for or against the perceiving country. The concept of neutrality becomes increasingly hard for the parties to believe in—the world is viewed as being almost polarised into the extreme positions.

None of these tendencies are, of course, unique to crisis situations. However, a characteristic of crisis situations is that the tendencies which can be seen to exist in any international situation where there is hostility are strengthened, often to a considerable degree. The whole process can, in fact, be described as one in which the decision-makers, whom one would normally expect to be relatively sophisticated, adopt progressively less and less sophisticated attitudes as the crisis develops. This is particularly unfortunate as it is is in times of tension, when decisions might have fateful consequences, that clear, sophisticated analysis is particularly desirable. The hardening of attitudes is one of the causes of escalation in crisis situations.

The other grouping of the characteristics of perceptions about a situation, as far as the decision-makers are concerned, involves the freedom of decision available. This is not so much a perception of the other decision-maker as of the decision-making environment as a whole. Perhaps the most significant characteristic of the situation is that the alternatives available appear to narrow as the situation becomes more tense. The decision-makers see the situation as one in which they are almost the tools of circumstance, and the decisions they can legitimately make become narrowly circumscribed, giving them little room for manoeuvre. This, of course, can easily lead to an amplification of the crisis, simply because there is no longer a search for alternatives, particularly heterodox ones. If one's own field of choice is narrowly circumscribed, then the situation can be remedied only by an action of the other side. However, if the other side feels similarly, then nothing is done to break away from what appears to be a preordained pattern—usually with adverse results.

With the feeling of being constrained in decision, comes a reduction in the care with which the effects of potentially violent acts are evaluated. Decisions are made emotionally, without rational consideration of the potentialities of the situation from a strategic point of view. Further, the rewards of violence are seen as greater, and the dangers of delay in initiating a military programme as more serious than in times of less stress. Strategic caution dwindles, and the advocates of military vigour begin to dominate—in now familiar terms, the hawks gain influence and the doves are ignored.

The crucial points which emerge in any analysis of crisis are that behaviour under crisis conditions is different from normal behaviour and is consistent with our general knowledge of groups under stress; and, from this, that a theory of crisis behaviour is quite possible, and indeed is close to being formulated. Such a theory is a pre-requisite for the effective control of crisis situations, such that the escalation process is halted and de-escalation initiated. This is of crucial importance in preventing the violent resolution of conflicts. Further, this is an area where the traditional tools of the social sciences, or at least variants of them which do not require extensive methodological development, can be applied. Our knowledge of crises may be elementary but it is not rudimentary, and the lines of development are much clearer than they are in other aspects of the discipline. Here, if anywhere, there could be rapid pay-offs from the scientific study of the subject.

chapter eight

The Theory of Arms Races

1 The Purpose of a Theory of Arms Races

The term 'arms race' is used to describe a situation where two or more countries increase their armaments in response to increases in the other country's arms, because of the threat they believe to be involved. This is a positive feedback process in which the actions of one country cause a reaction in another, which induces the first country to extend the scale of its actions, and so on.

Arms races have constantly troubled people who are interested in the problems of peace and war. The reasons for this are not hard to find. If two countries are continuously increasing their armaments, the likelihood of war would seem to increase. We shall discuss this question later, but its relevance to the study of peace and war is obvious. That arms races are a real phenomenon and not just a figment of the pacifists' imagination is clear[37]. One classic example is that of the naval race between Britain and Germany in the period before the first world war. Britain and Germany were enlarging their fleets, at times rather dramatically, by building, among other things, the large Dreadnoughts; and the explicit motivation in the case of both countries was the naval build-up of the other power. In more recent times, the Soviet Union and the United States have been increasing their nuclear armaments and accompanying delivery systems in response to the armaments of the other. There have been many other cases.

What is the function of a theory of arms races? The basic idea is to be able to specify the relationship between the armaments programme of two competing countries more precisely than by the rather loose type of statement contained in the first paragraph of this chapter. If we can do this, then we can go on and analyse the implications of such relationships in some detail. It is tempting, when thinking in general terms of an armaments race, to suppose that it would go on indefinitely, and that the nations would build up to progressively larger and larger levels of arms. We shall see that this is not necessarily true. The analysis of even simple relationships gives us an insight into some rather curious features of arms races which are by no means self-evident. It can, though it need not, lead us into some understanding of when and how armaments races stop.

The specification of explicit forms of the relationship between the arms levels of two countries also provides us with a tool for recognizing those elements which cause 'true' arms races in the sense that the primary motivation is fear of the arms level of some opposing power, and to what extent the arms build-ups are for some different purpose, for example, as a response to pressure-group interests. This unfortunately, is not easy. Arms races proceed only for a relatively small number of years and, as decisions are often made annually, there are usually only a very few observations of the system to go on. Results must be stated with only a limited degree of confidence.

Arms races are clearly relevant to war and, as such, are a proper part of the analysis of the causes of war. A theory of the arms race is not in itself, however, a theory of the causes of war. To connect it with these causes, we need a separate theory relating the level of armaments to the probability of war. This involves other questions, which we discuss below.

2 The Richardson Theory of Arms Races

While there has been much discussion of arms races in various contexts, particularly since the first world war, there has been remarkably little attempt to theorise about them. Social events which recur usually tempt some social scientist to construct a general theory of them, but arms races have been subjected only to historical description or, at the other extreme, dogmatic but inadequately substantiated statements of their effects. As in so many other parts of his field, the first serious attempt to theorise about arms races was by L. F. Richardson[6]. Subsequent work on the theory has followed fairly closely the pattern which he pioneered.

In this section, we shall describe a simplified version of the Richardson theory of the arms race which illustrates clearly its important characteristics.

Let us suppose that Paflagonia and Crim Tartary consider each other to be military rivals on the international scene. Each country views the arms of its opponent as directed against him and as requiring some response. Initially, let us assume that the sole factors which influence the Paflagonian government in setting its armaments level are the level of arms held by Crim Tartary, and an innate suspicion factor which means that they want a certain quantity of arms even if Crim Tartary has none at all. The higher Crim Tartary sets its armaments level, then the more arms Paflagonia★ requires above this point.

★ The use of the anthropomorphic view of the state nominally implied in such phrases as 'Paflagonia thinks that . . .' is one of the cardinal sins in the analysis of international relations. More appropriate terms would be 'The decision makers of Paflagonia think that . . .' It is, however, convenient to use the anthropomorphic version for brevity, while drawing attention to its dangers.

We can draw a simple graph of the level of arms which Paflagonia regards as the minimum acceptable in the face of any level possessed by Crim Tartary. The graph below illustrates a situation where Paflagonia requires at least £100 m worth of arms plus 80% of Crim Tartary's arms. Any point on or above the line which is drawn will mean that Paflagonia is satisfied, and regards itself as safe.

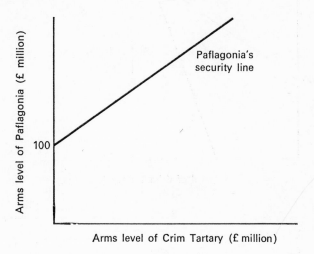

Figure 8.1

We can assume that Crim Tartary reacts in the same way, and regards it as necessary to have at least £110 m worth of arms plus 70% of Paflagonia's arsenal. Crim Tartary's safety level can similarly be drawn on a graph, it being regarded by Crim Tartary as necessary to be either on the security line or to the right of it. In Figure 8.2(a) we have superimposed the two security lines on the same graph.

These two lines divide the diagram into four areas, labelled P, Q, R and S. In areas P and Q, which lie to the left of Crim Tartary's security line, that country will be dissatisfied and will increase its arms level. This is represented in the diagram by a move towards the right. In areas Q and R, Paflagonia will be dissatisfied, and the consequent increase in its arms is represented by a move upwards in the graph. So, in area Q, both parties are increasing their arms and the general direction is therefore diagonally upwards. In area S, both sides are content and there is no alteration in the arms level. In P, the move is, of course, simply horizontal as Paflagonia has no desire to increase its arms levels. Correspondingly, in area R the move is vertically upwards.

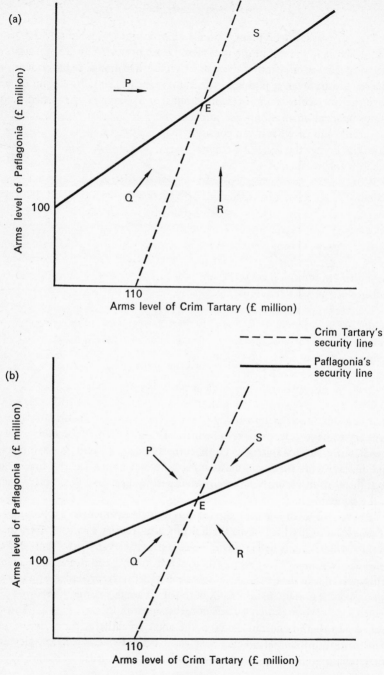

Figure 8.2

This is a very simple situation, and it will be worth complicating it a little before analysing the implications of such assumptions. While the quantity of an opponent's armaments is clearly a significant factor in determining a country's arms level, it is equally clearly not the only one. We shall add a factor which works in the opposite direction. Money spent on armaments cannot be spent on anything else, and a country which is arming is therefore poorer in terms of what it can consume than it would have been otherwise. Thus, the higher the level of a country's arms, the less enthusiastic is it likely to be for further increases.

We now have two factors, cost and security, pulling against each other and suggesting opposite courses of action. This makes for two modifications of the model. Consider the case of the Paflagonians, who do not really feel safe unless they have £100 m of armaments plus 80% of the level of Crim Tartary's arms. This, however, is costly, so they accept a security line equivalent to 70% of Crim Tartary's arms, feeling that the resources thus released for higher consumption are worth the cost of a little increase in insecurity. So Paflagonia's security line now has a rather lower slope (Figure 8.2(b)).

The second modification has a more significant effect on the theory itself. In the earlier version, Paflagonia did not really mind if it was above its security line, as this just meant that it had some superfluous arms. However, Paflagonia is now conscious of the added cost involved, and wishes to maintain just that level it needs, and no more. If, for some reason, Paflagonia finds itself above its security line, then it will reduce its level of arms until it falls back to the security level. This is illustrated in Figure 8.2 (b). If the arms levels are in area Q, both Paflagonia and Crim Tartary will be dissatisfied and will increase armaments—there will be an arms race. In area R, Paflagonia will feel insecure and increase its arms; Crim Tartary, however, will have too many and, finding them too costly, will cut back. In area P the converse will be the case. In area S, both will find the level of armaments too expensive and both will reduce them.

The treatment of rearmament and disarmament as reverse processes, each of which is equally likely, might seem glib in a world apparently more used to the former, except in periods of traumatic relief after a major war. Some caution is required, however, in interpreting the meaning of disarmament. Although disarmament sometimes takes the form, usually as a result of an agreement, of actually scrapping useful items of equipment and cutting down armed forces, there can be *de facto* disarmament simply by not replacing old and obsolete equipment. In this inconspicuous and rather negative form, disarmament is probably more common than is realised. Rearmament involves positively acquiring equipment or expanding forces (and spending more money), and is therefore more likely to attract attention. The theory does, indeed, regard the two processes as symmetrical, but, although this is a simplification, it is a more reasonable one than it might appear at first sight.

This picture of an armaments race is, of course, still absurdly simple. Despite this simplicity, it is worth analysing the implications of the assumptions we have made, as the results, in certain cases, are somewhat surprising.

The first question is whether there is some level of armaments at which neither country would want either to increase or decrease its amount of arms. This would be the 'balance of terror' point. Such a situation exists where the security lines of the two countries intersect (Figure 8.2, point E). At that point, each country is on its own security line, so the situation stays stable until some other factor alters. This point is called the *equilibrium arms level.*

We must next ask what happens when the actual level of armaments is not at the equilibrium arms level. This has been loosely considered in Figure 8.2 (b), but needs amplifying. Let us take a point F in Figure 8.3, between the security levels, and below the point of equilibrium.

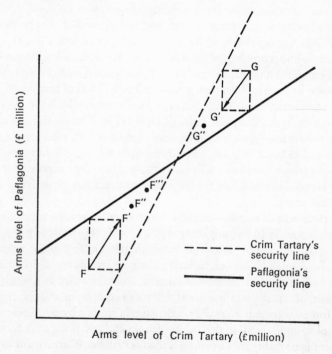

Figure 8.3

Each country is below its security level and therefore wants to increase its arms, Paflagonia by moving upwards in the diagram, and Crim Tartary by a move to the right. Let us assume for convenience that Paflagonia ignores the fact that Crim Tartary is also out of equilibrium, and increases its arms to its security level, assuming that the level of arms held by Crim Tartary will remain constant. Let Crim Tartary reason similarly. If they then simultaneously increase their arms by the appropriate amount, they will find themselves at point F', which is nearer the equilibrium but which still leaves them both dissatisfied. If the process is repeated, they will move successively to F", F''', and so on, until they reach the equilibrium point. Once there, of course, they will stop. If the hypothesis about the way the two countries decide on the arms increase in each year is correct, then the arms race will decrease in momentum year by year as the equilibrium is approached. However, not to allow for the rival's movement until it has occurred presupposes a certain amount of naïveté on the part of the rulers of the countries concerned. In practice, the error is more likely to be in the opposite direction, consisting of an over-estimate of the rival's hostile actions. However, the basic point, that the arms race will move continuously towards the equilibrium, is unaffected by this; the only change is in the path by which it moves there and the speed at which it approaches equilibrium.

Now let us take the point G which is also between the two security levels but is above the equilibrium point. In this case exactly the reverse process will take place. Because of the cost, both parties will move down towards their security level and, if we make the assumption that both sides ignore the possibility of the other decreasing its arms level, they will arrive at point G'. At the next stage, they will move to point G", and so on, until they get to the equilibrium level. Thus, although they will have mutually disarmed, this will not lead to a general and complete disarmament. The same sort of argument can be used to show that the countires will move to the equilibrium level of armaments from any other point on the diagram.

This sort of system, which moves to an equilibrium level no matter from where it starts, is said to possess a point of *stable equilibrium*. This is clearly not the same as saying that there is no arms race, but the very fact that it is limited (albeit possibly at a high level) is important.

Now let us look at another set of security curves, which are also permitted by our overall assumptions and which are illustrated in Figure 8.4. The critical differences between these lines and those in the first example are that Paflagonia's security line intersects the horizontal axis and is steeper than Crim Tartary's, which cuts the vertical axis. In the previous case, the reverse was true.

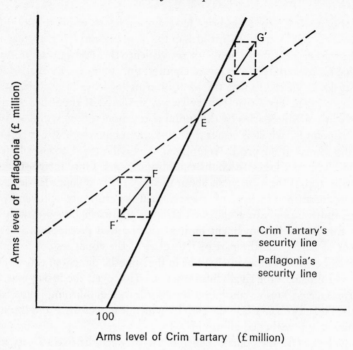

Figure 8.4

This is not as implausible as it might appear at first sight. The Government of Paflagonia is aware that Crim Tartary has various ends in view other than an attack on Paflagonia. It may, for example, have internal security problems for which it requires arms. Consequently, Paflagonia is content to be completely disarmed providing Crim Tartary does not have armaments in excess of £100 m. However, if Crim Tartary goes beyond this level, then Paflagonia reacts sharply. Thus an increase of, say, £100 m in Crim Tartary's arms provokes an increase of about £150 m in Paflagonia's (Figure 8.4). An equivalent assumption is made about Crim Tartary's reaction behaviour. In this new situation, as in the earlier case, there is an equilibrium level of arms indicated by the point E.

Now consider what happens when the arms levels are at a point F. Here, Paflagonia is above its security level and Crim Tartary is to the right of its line. Thus, both parties are anxious to reduce their armaments. By an analogous argument to the one conducted earlier, we can calculate that they will get to F'. This puts them both in a position even further away from their security levels. Consequently, they will reduce their armaments again, continuing in this way until they reach a completely disarmed state. The number of stages depends, of course, on how near they were to the actual equilibrium at the start of the process.

Now let us repeat the analysis, starting at point G, which is above the equilibrium position. Here, both Paflagonia and Crim Tartary are below their security level, and want to increase their arms. Again making our naïve behaviour assumption about how they arrange their arms levels, it is clear that, with each move that they make (to G′, etc.), they both fall further below their security levels. In consequence they will both again increase their armaments and move further yet from the equilibrium level, and there is no reason for the process to stop. They have therefore got themselves into a runaway arms race which has no limiting point, at least within the assumptions of the theory. Perhaps it will end in war, or perhaps in a dramatic revision, on the part of the countries concerned, of their conceptions of adequate security levels—the theory gives us no help on this point. Similar arguments can be carried out for the remaining areas, though with a qualification. From any point north east of the equilibrium point, but outside the area we have already considered, the arms movement would be into the explosive area. From any point south west of E, it will move down to zero. From any point north west or south east of the equilibrium point, it could move into either area and possibly to the equilibrium point. The equilibrium point has no particular attraction in this area, however, and the arrival of the arms system at this point would be pure coincidence.

In both the cases we have discussed, it has been assumed that an equilibrium level of arms actually exists. There is no particular reason for this, however. For instance, the two security levels could look as in Figure 8.5, the lines intersecting at a point where the armaments of the two powers are negative. This, of course, has no meaning, at least on our present definition of the variables. However, the situation poses no severe problem from the point of view of analysis. In case (a), any level of arms is unstable with respect to the hypothetical equilibrium point, and an indefinite arms race takes place. In the second case, the situation is stable, and the two countries will disarm completely, thus getting as near as possible to the equilibrium point.

The fact that the equilibrium is unobtainable does not mean that we cannot use it in the anlysis of those points which are obtainable. Indeed, the argument from which we derive the propositions about the behaviour of arms could be stated in terms which never mention this equilibrium at all. However, it is more convenient to state the issue in a general form and to regard all the situations as special cases, than to have a whole set of *ad hoc* situations.

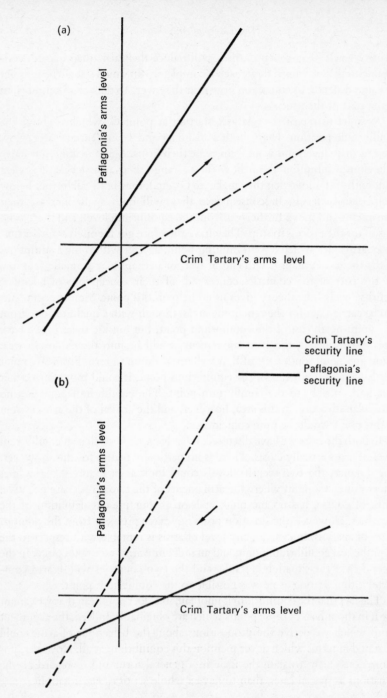

Figure 8.5

Before going on to discuss the significance of the Richardson theory, let us summarise the position so far. By making some simple assumptions about the factors which affect a country's decision concerning its arms level, we have shown that there are two principal groups of possible situations: first, when the arms system moves either up or down towards an equilibrium point at which the two parties no longer want either to increase or decrease their arms; and secondly, a system which has the curious feature of admitting both the possibility of a fully-fledged, unlimited arms race and, alternatively, complete mutual disarmament. These should be distinguished, at least in principle.

These conclusions are interesting and would be unlikely to emerge from a purely verbal analysis of the problem. Our ruthless simplification of the world's complexities has already begun to pay some dividends and, in the next section, we shall see to what extent these turn out to be illusory.

3 Some Implications of the Richardson Theory

Social systems are always in a state of flux, so we could not expect the security lines depicted in the Richardson model to remain stationary indefinitely. The lines on the graphs will, in fact, continually be moving around, and the suitability of the model as the basis for a theory of arms races depends on how severe such movements are. If the lines are continually jumping up and down, this is an indication that there are other important factors whose neglect seriously limits the usefulness of the theory. If, however, the movements are relatively small, the model can form a suitable basis for a theory, and we can begin to analyse the problem in these terms.

Suppose, for the moment, that the world is such that the model, by and large, represents accurately real arms races, but that there are some moderate variations in the lines. What significance would this have for the student of arms races?

As far as the stable case is concerned, the model is quite well-behaved. Suppose that an arms race with security lines P_1 and C_1 is going on, and that it is approaching the equilibrium point E_1 where it will stop (Figure 8.6). Now imagine that, for some reason, the two countries get more sensitive to each other's level of arms and the old pair of lines are replaced by P_2 and C_2 which establish a new, higher equilibrium point at E_2.

The arms levels will move towards the new equilibrium and, if it changes, the system will run after it. The general situation will be more or less unaltered.

In the unstable case, the increase in the sensitivity of the two countries is represented, for Crim Tartary, by a line to the right of the original one, and

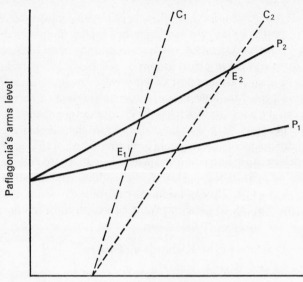

Figure 8.6

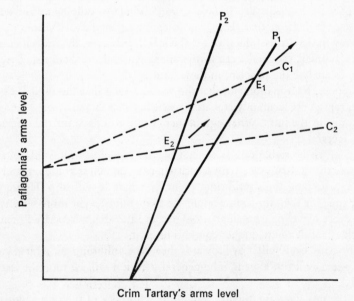

Figure 8.7

for Paflagonia, by a line above the old one, as in the stable situation. However, in this case, the effect of the increased sensitivity is to produce a lower equilibrium point than before, which appears slightly paradoxical (Figure 8.7). Suppose now, that the actual level of arms at some time is below the equilibrium point in an unstable system. The system will be heading away from the equilibrium towards complete disarmament. If there is an increase in sensitivity to the rival's arms, the equilibrium point might be lowered so that the existing arms level is above it, thus reversing the trend and causing a run-away arms race. Relatively minor alternations in the system could produce this effect—or, indeed, the opposite. In an unstable system, it is clear that relatively small variations in the constants of the system can produce dramatically different results—which is why it is called an unstable system. Clearly, in such situations policy decisions have to be made with great caution, as an action might have quite unexpected consequences.

4 Arms Races and War

A theory of arms races is not, in itself, a theory of the cause of war. Wars do not start simply because of the mutual hostility engendered by an arms build-up. What is necessary to connect the two is an explicit theory which relates levels of arms to the likelihood of war. This can be built onto the theory of the arms race to give a comprehensive picture of the whole process.

To state that arms races are the cause of war is, in any case, a loose formulation of the problem. The statement might mean that all wars are preceded by arms races—i.e. that an arms race is a necessary condition for war. This is easy to refute. Alternatively, it could mean that all arms races are followed by wars—i.e. that an arms race is a sufficient, but not a necessary, condition for war. In point of fact, we are unlikely to seek a proposition as rigorous as either of these, but would modify the statement by a phrase such as 'more often than not'. In other words, we would enunciate statistical propositions, suggesting, for instance, that arms races predispose nations to war rather than necessarily precipitating it.

There are various theories which relate the quantity of arms to the likelihood of war. Some of these emphasize the destabilising effects of arms, and others argue that, under certain conditions, arms are stabilising factors. We shall state two of these theories in an extreme form. On the one hand, there is the theory which Richardson seems, by implication, to support: that war gets more likely, the more arms there are. The concern here is with the total quantity of arms held by both powers, the distribution between them being seen as of minor significance. The opposite extreme is where the over-all level of arms is thought not to be important, what matters being the balance between the two powers involved. In this case, if there is a balance of terror (it is important to differentiate this from a balance of power, which is a situation where there are several countries which can switch alliances), then there is little danger of war, as it would be equally costly to both sides.

Few people hold either of these theories in the extreme forms stated. In fact, the differences in view-point are more a matter of emphasis than a complete denial of the validity of the other point of view. One can therefore quite easily hold a theory which combines elements of both, arguing that the probability of war increases if an imbalance grows up between the contending powers, that this is aggravated if the level of arms is high and, further, that, even if a balance exists, the probability of war increases as this balance moves up to higher and higher levels. A balance, incidentally, should not be equated with an equilibrium point of the arms race theory, but should be interpreted as being something like equality of arms. However, as the equilibrium is defined as the point where both parties are satisfied, it would seem likely, in addition, to be a balance of terror point if the statesmen of the countries concerned held some version of the balance theory.

Now, the relationship between the quantity of arms and the likelihood of war is, in principle, an empirical one, that is one which can be settled, or at least illuminated, by reference to what has actually happened. Unfortunately, in practice, this is a much more difficult undertaking as very little systematic, comparative information, on arms races has been collected. There are a few individual arms races which are reasonably well documented. The obvious examples are the classic arms races preceding the first and second world war. There are others, slightly less well known, such as those between France and the North German Federation from 1868 to 1870, between Russia and Turkey, from 1872 to 1877, and between Russia and Japan from 1901 to 1904. All except the present contest were succeeded by wars, but, for a proper analysis, one would need to examine much more thoroughly the cases where arms races were not followed by wars. These are less likely to be remembered as they are less spectacular, but only after a very diligent search would we be justified in concluding that such situations were rare. Unfortunately, this diligent search has not been carried out to date, though it is clearly a very important task. Until the question has been examined more thoroughly, we cannot begin to decide whether arms races as such are a serious predisposing factor towards war.

We can, however, do a little better in examining the hypothesis that wars are usually preceded by arms races. Of the 84 wars which ended between 1820 and 1929, only 10 were preceded by arms races which have been asserted to be a cause[7]. The analysis, however, is rather shaky, as some of the remaining 74 wars were preceded by arms races, and it is conceivable that there was a causal element some of these other situations. A more detailed investigation might give arms races a greater significance, though, on the basis of the evidence currently available, it seems doubtful that the hypothesis that war is normally a result of an arms race will be substantiated.

One configuration of security lines in the Richardson theory results in a run-away arms race. If we are correct in suggesting that arms races are relatively rarely the principal cause of war, does it mean that this explosive version is rarely found? The answer is that it does not. If we followed an explosive arms race to its supposedly logical conclusion, we would get the absurd result of both sides having indefinitely large quantities of arms. However, we do not suppose that real life behaves indefinitely in this manner, but rather that it is necessary to seek some extension of the theory which will eliminate the theoretical possibility which we know to be a practical impossibility. In the case of the explosive arms race, there are two obvious possibilities, namely war and economic poverty.

Economic impoverishment due to an arms race seems rare, but a modified version of it may not be. It is possible that, as costs grow, their dampening effects increase more than proportionately after some point (Fig. 8.8). There

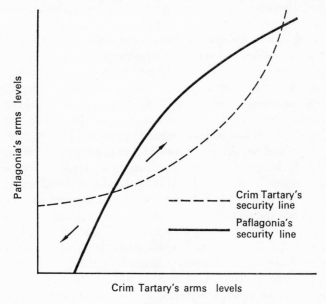

Figure 8.8

may, in fact, be an upper ceiling on the proportion of the national income which a country will spend on arms, unless it is actually at war. This may be short of what would produce what could reasonably be called impoverishment. This suggests that the instability of the explosive arms race may, in certain cases, be localised by the existence of some upper stable equilibrium point to which it would ultimately tend—though this might, of course, involve a high level of arms.

5 Difficulties and Extensions

The real world does not look very much like the world depicted in the model of arms races—it is much more complicated. What then is the point in analysing it as if it did? There are two points to make in response to this, both of them negative. First, we have shown that intuition is a very poor guide to reaching an understanding of a situation. Without formulating a model and putting it into simple mathematical terms, it is very unlikely that we should have come across the division of possibilities into stable and unstable systems, where the latter in particular has such peculiar characteristics. At its very weakest, this model has demonstrated that unstable systems are possible and that small alterations in the current situation do not always have small results but sometimes dramatically big ones. This theory, though undoubtedly very much simplified, has a measure of plausibility. The fact that instabilities can occur in such simple systems destroys one's confidence in the stability of more realistic and complex systems. Complexity by itself does not make the system any more stable; in fact, the reverse tends to be true. There may be more balancing factors, but there may also be more destabilising factors.

The second response, which is implicit in what was said in the first chapter of this book, is that many events which are affected by a large number of factors can, nevertheless, be predominantly explained by a few. Arms races have still not been sufficiently examined for us to say with certainty whether this is true of them or not. The Richardson theory could be deficient either because it is too simple, or, alternatively, because it seized on the wrong variables. The tests of the Richardson theory are still not extensive. Richardson himself applied the theory to the period before 1914 and to the inter-war period, and Smoker[38] has applied it to the post-war arms race between the U.S.A. and the U.S.S.R. Neither test establishes that the theory in its original or a modified form really is satisfactory, though nor do these tests indicate conclusively that something like the theory is inapplicable. We still have to be open-minded. However, the claim that, because the theory is simple, it is worthless is invalid. A number of types of social event are much simpler on examination than they appear at first sight, and the arms race may be one of them.

The theory of the arms race has been analysed in mathematical terms. The point of doing so is not, as is sometimes hinted, to make it more difficult to understand. Apart from the fact that it is frequently easier to work out a theory initially in mathematical terms, even though it may subsequently prove quite possible to express it in ordinary verbal language, there is the point that, using mathematics, it is easier to see what the precise consequences of some assumptions really are. A set of completely plausible premises might turn out, on investigation, to yield extremely implausible implications. It is often much easier to see this in the highly disciplined mathematical language than in verbal discussions, which, being much more prone to ambiguity, are not always particularly suitable for expressing complex logical arguments.

The value of a mathematical argument is seen in the extension of the Richardson theory to an arms race between several nations. The two nation case is, of course, a great simplification as arms races often involve more countries. Common language is inadequate to describe the complexities involved, and mathematical forms have to be resorted to. There are many ways in which an arms race might involve more than two parties, and a general theory of arms races must be prepared to make provision for each. One possibility is a number of nations all arming against each other. Something like this seems to be happening between the Soviet Union, the United States, and China at the moment, especially with respect to nuclear weapons. This is a three cornered race, which could, in principle, be tackled in the same way as the simpler two party case we have considered, though the resulting theory looks more complicated.

Another variant of the arms race system occurs when there are several countries divided into two blocs. If all members of each bloc feel the same way as their partners, the problem can be dealt with in the same way as the two country arms race, blocs taking the place of countries. However, such similarity of interest is not likely to exist for very long. An approximation to this situation existed in the late forties and early fifties between the Western and Eastern alliances. Normally, though, a country in an alliance is unlikely to regard its allies' weapons as quite the equivalent of its own, not simply out of prejudice, but because it knows that there might be occasions when an ally would refuse to go to war, even if there were a general similarity of outlook between the two nations. Furthermore, countries feel threatened to different degrees by the rival alliance and are likely to react differently to their armaments. However, these problems can, to some extent, be treated as modifications of the two party arms race. A greater complication is the fact that the various countries in the blocs have interests elsewhere which also influence the level of arms they require. Thus, Britain in the post-war period has wanted arms for a variety of purposes other than because of its fears of the Soviet Union. One cannot explain the British arms level purely in Cold War terms.

A final extension of the theory is necessary when several arms races interact. One such situation is in the hostility between India and Pakistan, and also between India and China. Their mutual dislike of India has drawn China and Pakistan together, but Pakistan is also allied with the United States which is very hostile to China. We have, therefore, a set of relationships which, if they existed between individual people, would provide the basis for the plot of a novel. The India-Pakistan-China situation cannot be interpreted entirely in terms of an arms race hostility, but there are elements of it present. Pakistan expressed uneasiness at the armed preparations of India which were directed against China, fearing the weapons might subsequently be used against them.

The extension of the Richardson theory to arms races involving many countries is complicated, but it does not collapse beneath the weight. The theory can be broadened to encompass situations more closely reminiscent of the real world than the basic theory which has been dealt with here, in a manner which still retains the essential characteristics of the discussion.

A problem which occurs in the discussion of any theory of this kind which depends on measurement is how to carry out the quantification necessary. The essentials of this problem have been discussed in the first chapter, but it is also appropriate to discuss it with reference to the Richardson theory. The basic conclusions of the theory, that an arms race can be either stable or unstable, are true given a wide variety of different measures. Failure to find an appropriate one would not weaken its value as a cautionary tale, but, if we are to test and apply the theory, we need to find a suitable way of measuring the level of arms.

In the description of the theory, the level of arms was measured in terms of money spent on them. This is very crude—price levels change from country to country, and the rates of exchange used to compare currencies (particularly those such as the dollar and the rouble) have some arbitrary elements in them. Nevertheless, this measure, though crude, may be quite adequate for many purposes. However, as we are concerned with arms as devices for threatening nations, it would be more appropriate to take military effectiveness as the measure of the size of arms levels. Cost as a criterion conceals the fact that some forms of weapons are much more to be feared than others, in a manner which may not be closely related to cost. Some forms of arms may not be effective against certain countries—a land-locked country is unlikely to worry too much about another country's battleships (though it might about its aircraft carriers). Ways of measuring effectiveness are not impossible to derive, but they necessarily depend on many arbitrary assumptions.

The difficulties of formulating an effectiveness measure for arms levels are compounded when we recognise that it is not only the weapons which a country has which are of significance, but also those which it could acquire in the near future. For instance, the image of a completely disarmed state is more ambiguous than it appears at first sight. It seems legitimate to regard a disarmed country which could produce a nuclear bomb within a year as being 'less disarmed' than one which is not capable of producing such a weapon within the foreseeable future. Similar conditions apply to countries which are not in a completely disarmed state. Even looking at the measurement of arms levels from the cost side alone, there are many different possibilities. Another possibility apart from single money cost is the proportion of the national income which is spent on arms. The suggestion that Richardson put forward, with ingenuity but a lack of feel for the English language, was what he called 'warfinpersal'. This, rather roughly, is the amount of work-time spent on war-like pursuits (both within the armed forces and on the making of military equipment), the time being weighted for importance by salary. Thus an Air Marshal is regarded as equalling several Cooks Class II, the precise number being determined by their relative incomes. *Prima facie*, this is as good as any other measure. In such matters, there is no 'true measure', and one uses what is convenient and enables meaningful results to be derived.

Once again, the measurement problem is both serious and difficult to solve. It is not, none the less, a problem which invalidates the exercise, for even crude measures embodied in crude theories can, in many cases, be illuminating as guides to the behaviour of the world.

No one is claiming that the theory of the arms race depicted in this chapter solves the problem definitively. It very clearly does not. There are as many open questions at the end of the analysis as there were at the beginning. However, these are new questions, and the analysis of the problem in such a way that answers may be found is an achievement of great importance. The thorough investigation of arms races from a scientific point of view is still in its infancy, and this chapter has the standing of a pediatrician's report to the general public on the infant's progress; happily, the prognosis for a useful and healthy life for the theory seems excellent.

chapter nine

Experimental Methods—International Simulation

1 An Experimental Approach

It is a time-honoured maxim that experiment is impossible in the social sciences and even more so in history. Some small areas of psychology might be excluded from this restriction, but even there the limitations of the method are so severe that it may be illegitimate to extrapolate from peoples' behaviour in a psychological laboratory to that in their normal life. It is argued that results in this field are trivial when valid, or, if important, are not readily susceptible to laboratory experimentation. In the accepted sense of the word, experimentation on social systems is usually out of the question. No Chancellor of the Exchequer or Minister of Finance is going to adopt the suggestion of an economist just to see what happens. Nor is a Foreign Secretary likely to follow some policy merely to satisfy the curiosity of an empirically minded political scientist.

The obvious sense of the word 'experiment' is not, however, the only sense. If experiment on a social system is impossible for a whole variety of practical reasons, it is still sometimes possible to do experiments on some other system which, in some ways, resembles the social system which is the primary object of interest. One can, in principle, derive information from the observation of an experimental social group, and this can be applied, possibly with modification, to another social group on whom experiment is impossible. This is not an activity used only in the social sciences; it is, in fact also practised in the natural sciences, as will be illustrated later.

The suggestion that it might be possible to apply experimental results to the analysis of the behaviour of states is of recent origin. As with everything else in this field, there is always the danger that a data-hungry analyst of the international system might see group experimentation as the panacea which will solve all his problems. It is very doubtful that experiments are a panacea, but it seems probable that they will prove helpful. The case for this point of view will be argued in this chapter.

The experiments which have been run and which are of interest to the student of the behaviour of states fall into two groups which lie at opposite ends of the spectrum of complexity. On one hand, there are the *simulations* where a situation is set up which reproduces as closely as possible the international decision-making environment. A number of teams, whose functions are to act the part of a government in some given decision making context, are arranged. The members of the teams are then allocated particular roles, such as that of Prime Minister or Foreign Secretary, and instructed to 'play' accordingly. These simulations, when they involve human subjects, are frequently misleadingly referred to as 'games'. The aim of this approach is to gain some understanding of the real situation by examining a simplified but still complex model of it.

At the other extreme of the experimental spectrum are very simple games played between two people, where the choices available to them are very tightly constrained, frequently being restricted to two[22]. These games make no pretence of reproducing real situations, the aim being to gain an understanding of some aspects of behaviour in the hope that the knowledge may be transferable to more complex situations.

There have been experiments conducted at intermediate levels of complexity, but usually in some other context than international relations[39]. They have an interest for us, for they seem a fruitful line of attack, which will presumably be taken up in the international relations field at some stage. However, we shall discuss them only peripherally, confining ourselves mainly to complex simulations[40, 41]. The application of the results from simple games is bound to be indirect, whereas complex simulations have the prospect of being more directly applicable.

International affairs is not the only area in which the technique of gaming is used, and, indeed, it is a relatively new area of application. Moreover, the technique itself is not particularly new.

War gaming, for instance, is a time-honoured exercise. Chess may owe its origins to a war game. Naval games are played with ships on a large board, the fighting characteristics of the ships being specified. Tactical army games can be played in a similar way. The 'exercises' which the various services go through are, in effect, games. For the most part, war games are played as training, the indoor kind being usually for decision takers, while the outdoor variety are partly for this purpose and partly to accustom the lower levels of the military organisations to waiting about for long periods in the cold prior to being badly frightened. Sometimes there is a research element in all this. In the indoor games, one can use imaginary equipment with characteristics superior to those of available weapons to see what the advantages of these characteristics are. However, the main purpose of the exercise is usually training in one form or another.

Business games are closer in structure to international games. The participants are divided into teams and are allocated roles within the team such as General Manager, Finance Officer and Sales Director. One of the more sophisticated of these games is that played at the Graduate School of Industrial Administration at the Carnegie-Mellon University [42]. Here, students are divided into three teams and presented with information about their firms in a market which loosely corresponds to the characteristics of the detergent market in the United States. They are then obliged to make monthly decisions about the whole host of matters which the real decision-taker would have to consider in such a situation—the level and location of inventory, cash reserves, prices, etc. The decisions of the various firms are then fed into a computer and the sales, profits and so on come out, becoming the data for the ensuing month. The students play a series of months under this system. The game is primarily a training tool and, as such, is reasonably effective. It research potential has been less thoroughly explored to date.

Gaming simulations are not oddities thought up by wild-eyed eccentrics. The technique has a perfectly respectable history as a training device, and the sponsors of such activities must believe that the gaming situation has a good deal in common with the real situation. If this is so, then the game might actually provide new insights into the real situation. This possibility is now being explored by an increasing number of investigators.

2 A Description of Some Games

The nature of gaming can best be understood if some actual games are described. We shall discuss two which have been run, one being a game based on an actual historical event, and the other a more general purpose game which represents a fictitious world, but which can also be adapted to model real situations.

The first is the Bosnian crisis game run at the University of Lancaster, and the other is the Internation Simulation (usually abbreviated to INS) which has been developed at Northwestern University in the U.S.A. The reasons for selecting these two are that the author was responsible for the Bosnian game, and is therefore intimately familiar with it, while the INS game is the earliest of the present generation of games and also the most thoroughly investigated. The two games are also different in their basic design, which makes a comparison useful.

The Bosnian Crisis Game: The real-life background to this game is the Balkans in 1909. During 1908, Austria-Hungary annexed Bosnia-Herzegovina. The territory had been under Austrian control for some time, but it had technically belonged to the Turks who, however, were pacified by the

£2 million offered in exchange for a *de jure* recognition of the *de facto* situation. The country most perturbed by all this was Serbia, which had itself wanted the provinces, and who also suspected (not without some justification) that Austria's ambitions extended further afield, and might in the end include Serbia itself. The various European powers aligned themselves around the dispute. Germany, in particular, supported Austria-Hungary, and Russia, whose Foreign Minister was angered and embarrassed by the failure of Austria-Hungary to keep an illicit agreement (made in violation of the Treaty of London of 1871) under which Russia would get access through the Dardanelles in exchange for recognition of the annexation, supported Serbia. The crisis simmered gently throughout 1908, but in early 1909 it escalated sharply and, for a period in March, it seemed quite possible that it would end in a European war. On March 23rd 1909, the Germans sent a barely disguised ultimatum to Russia, to the effect that it should keep out of the Balkans. After some initial dithering, the crisis was resolved by Russia climbing down.

In the gaming version, the participants were given a history of the actual events up to the German ultimatum, after which they responded as they thought fit.

Normally there were seven teams, each with about four players. There was also a control team whose function consisted of administering the game and intervening if this proved necessary. The major physical activity was the sending of messages from one team to the other, which was done via the control team, who vetted it for plausibility (only rejecting it in extreme cases), recorded it, and then sent it off to the team to which it was supposed to go. It was also possible for a team to make some sort of military move, such as to mobilise its reserves or move troops. This was also done by sending a message to the control team which notified the other teams after what seemed like a plausible delay, unless the acting team had done so itself. Each team, of course, had the necessary information about its armed forces, the speed at which they could be raised or moved and so on. Further information could always be demanded from the control team.

In this way, the teams generated their own history of the crisis—a fictitious history which, however, was based on an initially real situation and operated with realistic constraints.

A factor which is changed in a simulation as compared with reality is time. In principle, a crisis simulation could be played in real time so that a real day is represented by a day in the crisis. However, for practical reasons, time is compressed, so that, in the case of the Bosnian game, the time scale was one hour to one day. How sensitive simulations are to the reduction in time scale is not known.

The teams represented Austria-Hungary, Russia, Germany, Serbia, Britain, Italy and France. Each had a Head of State (for example, Edward VII in the case of Britain), a Head of Government, a Foreign Secretary and in one or two cases a Chief of Staff. There were slight variants of this for different countries (for example, in the rather peculiar case of Austria-Hungary, there were two Heads of Government, one for each), but the general pattern was of this form. Four or five people seems generally to be about the size of the primary decision-making group in a crisis such as this, so the small team approach was not unreasonable. Each team was put in a separate room so that there was no direct verbal communication between them, and so that they could decide on their policies without fear of being overheard. However, this introduces a probably distorting effect in that a small group taking a decision in one room inevitably tends to act as a committee, achieving consensus where possible and otherwise voting. The hierarchic features of real governmental decision-making groups, which are established more on the basis of a given role than on personality, are more or less lost. Furthermore, the decisions which are made by a small group in the same room are likely to be different from those taken by participants who are normally physically separated.

Following reality, none of the runs of the simulation resulted in war, though it is possible that one or two might have done if they had been allowed to go on longer. For practical reasons it is clearly often necessary to cut a simulation off rather arbitrarily. For the most part, the histories generated were plausible and, at least at a superficial level, it seems that the real crisis could have taken the direction taken by the game.

One serious criticism of a game which starts from an actual historical situation is that the participants have at least a rough knowledge of the development of the actual situation and may be tempted to imitate this. In a narrow sense this does not appear to have been the case, but it does seem to have mattered as far as some of the background attitudes were concerned. For example, the participants were aware of the nature of the first world war and assumed that any war which might have broken out amongst the same powers in 1909 would also have been on a very large scale, involving an incredible amount of killing. However, the decision-makers in the real situation probably thought of war on the pattern of the Franco-Prussian war of 1870, which did not involve anything like the same amount of bloodshed. This may have induced a greater caution amongst the players. A compensating fact was that the players in the simulation knew that the situation was not real and that, whatever happened, they could still go home for tea. However, it seems to be the almost universal experience of people who have carried out simulations that the participants get involved and take the decisions seriously, as if concerned about the consequences.

The Internation Simulation (INS): This game, developed in the late nineteen fifties at Northwestern University by Professor Harold Guetzkow [43], and his colleagues, was the first major attempt to simulate international behaviour on a large scale. Most subsequent work derives directly or indirectly from this and it is not really possible to talk of the simulation of international behaviour without reference to this pioneering project.

The purposes and design of the game are rather different from those of the Bosnian crisis game. The INS is primarily designed to simulate behaviour over years rather than days. Each playing period is of the order of seventy minutes and, in that period, the decisions appropriate to a year are taken. The format of the decisions is laid down, that is, a decision maker has to fill in a decision form which specifies certain questions that have to be answered within the constraints. Naturally, in view of the fact that years are involved, there is a range of questions which are not relevant in a shorter period simulation, where the game can be regarded almost exclusively as a question of the interaction between the states. Economic decisions such as 'guns or butter' choices must be made, and these are not readily variable over short periods. Because of this greater degree of complexity, there has to be imposed on the game a whole corpus of theory which is not acted out by the players in question. For example, in a game meant to simulate behaviour over years, it is necessary to build into the procedure some theory of how and when governments are replaced, either legitimately or by revolution. If every step were to be played by live players, the game would be unwieldy. The alternative is to have rules which state when a government needs to be replaced because it has failed to satisfy the 'electorate'. These rules can be of a greater or lesser degree of complexity, but depend on some hypothesis as to what keeps the country happy (or at least non-revolutionary), and to what extent a decision-maker is constrained by the opinions of the populace—something which clearly varies significantly from country to country. There are many of these rules so, at the end of every year, the over-all consequences of the decisions which have been made by the various teams are not self-evident. In the INS, a computer is used to evaluate the consequences of the various actions, and the results are then given to the decision-makers as the 'history' for them to act on in the next 'year'.

A simulation of events which take place over a long period must involve more variables than one which takes place over a short period. If the experimenter is interested in a particular social group (for example, the 'government') whose decisions are affected by a much wider social group, then, as for most purposes it would be impracticable to represent the latter in the simulation by people, such factors have to be plugged into the experimental system from outside. Thus, there must be a theory of those decision processes which affect, but are not part of, the focal point of the simulation. In the INS game, the theory of these other social processes is programmed into the computer and, unavoidably, the development of the simulation is, in part, dependent on the validity of this theory. However, the computer is a more consistent instrument than a human control team, which is viable in a short period simulation only because there need be less theory imposed.

The basic INS model has been used to simulate 'real' situations as well as the artificial ones for which it was originally designed. For instance, it was used in a project jointly operated by the Peace Research Centre in England and the Canadian Peace Research Institute to simulate the Vietnam War [44]. Extended time periods and decisions involving economic and other long-term variables were obviously appropriate for this purpose. The INS model was also used by Charles and Margaret Hermann to simulate the crisis which preceded the outbreak of the First World War [45]. This imposed something of a strain on the INS design, which was not really intended for such short-term situations. The problems of simulating the outbreak of the First World War were obviously rather similar to those involved in the Bosnian Crisis. However, as the events of the 1914 crisis were much better known than those of 1909, the danger that the participants in the game would simply 'act out' the crisis was correspondingly greater. This was partially overcome by 'masking' the events—making the circumstances similar but not identical to those of the real situation (subsequent questioning showed that many of the participants had, in fact, seen through this). As the Hermanns remark, the simulation of historical events for research, as distinct from teaching purposes, is probably better done on less well known situations. Then the advantage that there is a 'real' system against which to compare the simulated system is not counterbalanced by the difficulties of too much knowledge on the part of the participants.

A relative of the simulation of historical events is that of possible future events. An example of this approach is the Conex game run by M. H. Banks, A. J. R. Groom and A. N. Oppenheim, which is based on a hypothetical crisis in the Middle East in the near future. It does not involve a computer but, like the Bosnian Crisis Game, relies on a human control team.

The simulations so far described have all involved people, with or without computers. One important purpose of the simulations has been to study how people behave—how their perceptions alter and what they decide to do. We also want to know how the system as a whole behaves, and are interested in the conditions under which the participants will go to war. Alternatively, one may suppose that people respond in known or assumed ways to various conditions, and ask what is the outcome of these sets of decisions in a complex, interacting environment. Clearly, the mixed simulations partially answer this question. However, the problem is approached in a much more constrained and controlled way in all-computer simulations, where the decision rules are built into the model, and where some or all of them are not left 'free' as in those simulations involving people. The computer itself is not really relevant to the methodological issue involved. A simple model designed to investigate the consequences of decision-taking procedures can be worked out without the aid of computers (as most social science models until recently have been). The computer is involved only because we are dealing with a very complex model without which it is impracticable (but not, in principle, impossible) to work.

The aim of the exercise is to specify certain decision-rules for the participants and then to simulate the consequences of the use of these rules. A decision rule is a procedure which governs the decision taken on the basis of the circumstances and events (including the decisions of others) faced by the decision taker. For example, a very simple decision rule might be, 'If a perceived enemy mobilises, follow suit.' Another rule for a particular participant might be, 'If a perceived rival suggests a conference between principal powers, accept but modify the proposal by suggesting the inclusion of minor powers.' These are, perhaps, presented in an over-simplified form, but may give the flavour of the idea.

One can build up a model on the procedures suggested, and see how it works. The test of such a model is to see whether the 'history' generated by the interacting set of decisions parallels the history generated in real life. Thus one might allocate some decision rules to the participants in the 1914 crisis, build a model on this basis, and see if the computer crisis is essentially the same as the real one. If it is, then we can infer that the decision procedures fed into the model are, in fact, appropriate, and do describe the real procedures used in those circumstances. The simulation procedure is then a test of the theory of a crisis (or any other set of international decisions) implicit in the formulation of a set of decision rules.

One such simulation is the 'Criscom' model, formulated under the aegis of the Simulmatics Corporation by Ithiel de Sola Pool and his associates [46]. The fascination of the 1914 crisis is such that the model has inevitably been applied there. The aspect which has so far been the centre of study is the interaction of the Kaiser and the Czar, the cognitive processes of these two decision-makers being simulated according to various rules, some similar to those which have emerged from other crisis studies. For example, the simulated decision-maker is subject to two sorts of information filter: first, he does not get all the information, and secondly, there is a self-imposed filter which sifts out information that contradicts his preconceived view of the world. The decisions which arise as a consequence of this form of rule can be simulated on the computer, and the reaction of the system as a whole can be examined.

This form of simulation is obviously somewhat different from gaming. It is the examination of the behaviour of a system on the assumption that its constituent elements behave in specified ways. The test of whether the assumptions made are correct lies in the degree of correspondence between the system behaviour and the events being modelled.

Given that we have obtained a successful simulation, it then becomes possible to experiment with it by altering one or more of the behaviour rules and observing the consequences. The implied assumption is that there is a degree of independence between the behaviour rules and that the altering of one does not involve the altering of several others. Whether this is reasonable or not is, of course, ultimately a matter for judgement. The technique cannot establish beyond doubt that the system will behave in a particular manner if certain alterations are made; it can only predict its behaviour given that certain preconditions are observed.

There are many problems involved in this form of activity with which we shall not be concerned. Even in computer simulations generating statistical data, there are difficulties in defining when the correspondence between the simulated and the primary system is 'good' or 'adequate'. In a system in which much of the data is qualitative, this is even harder. However, these are problems of inference which can be studied, and the fact that there are problems does not invalidate the whole activity.

3 The Logic of Experiment

The simulations which have been described are clearly experiments of a sort, though not in the way in which the word is commonly understood. An experiment of any sort is a device for finding out something about the behaviour of the world. It is a form of observation, though in some sense it is an artificial observation. There are three forms of experimental observation as understood in the sciences. First, we can observe the real world as it actually is without interfering with its behaviour. Secondly, we can set up experiments (in the normally understood sense) designed to investigate the phenomena in which we are interested. We still observe the real world, but in an artificial environment. Thirdly, if it is impracticable, unethical or illegal to experiment on some structure, it is sometimes possible to work on another structure which is related in some relevant sense. The first of these classes of observation is not normally referred to as an experiment. The second is an experiment proper, and the third is a quasi-experiment, clearly different in some important respects from the second type. We shall deal with each of these in turn.

On the face of it, 'pure observation' would seem to be the most satisfactory. We are primarily interested in finding out about the 'real world', and the obvious method is to look at it. It is a widely practised technique. Astronomers cannot experiment on stars, so they must look at them as best they can (though they make extensive use of knowledge from physics, much of it based on experiments). Similarly, ethologists look at animals in the wild state to find out about their habits, it having been shown that conclusions about animal behaviour based on observations made in the artificial environment of a zoo are seriously misleading. Sociologists gather data from people, and historians similarly observe actual events (as far as they can tell) rather than an artificial environment. The drawbacks of this approach are often serious, however. The real world is very complex, and even sophisticated statistical methods are not always adequate to sort out the patterns of information. Secondly, and perhaps more importantly, a lot of information is quite simply unobtainable. This is particularly true for the historian interested in decision-making. When a Cabinet takes a decision, it normally does so in secret, without outside observers. Subsequent reports are made by people from memory (which is both notoriously defective and selective), frequently with the aim of self-justification. Information about such decision-making processes is therefore likely to be seriously deficient and not always very reliable. This is even more true of informal decision-making processes, such as the doubtless very significant discussions which take place in private between senior decision-makers. The understanding of decision-making processes is crucially important if we are to comprehend the behaviour of the international system, but it is an area where the results of simple observation are seriously defective.

The experiment proper is widely used in the physical sciences. If a chemist is interested in the chemical properties of some substance, he can isolate it from the over-all environment and subject it to variations in one or two specific variables, for example temperature, and see the effect of this on its own. In this way, he can test a narrower range of properties, at one time, than would be possible if he were confined to observing the behaviour of the chemical in a 'natural state'. The psychologist carries out experiments on human beings, asking them to do various things in artificial and simplified environments of a type they are unlikely to find in their normal lives. Thus a considerable amount of work has been done on gambling by offering experimental subjects a large number of simplified gambles. From these experiments, we know quite a lot about how people behave in this very stylised conflict situation. The problem is how to transfer the knowledge gained from the simplified situation into the complicated real world.

Here the natural scientists have had a wide degree of success, at least in the 'classical' natural sciences such as physics and chemistry. For example, a knowledge of the theory of gravitation and the behaviour of large masses of fluids enables very accurate propositions to be made about the tides, even though it is obviously impossible to do many experiments on the tides themselves. There are other areas where the procedure is less satisfactory—there is, for instance, a vast difference in both accuracy and precision between meteorological and astronomical predictions. Nevertheless, on balance, the natural scientists can claim a substantial measure of success in overcoming the transference problem. The same is not true of the limited number of experiments which can be done in the social and behavioural sciences. Though we do know a great deal about behaviour in the Prisoners' Dilemma, we have very little idea of how to use these results in making propositions about the real world. It seems likely that what will happen will be a building up from simple to complex experiments, to see what behaviour patterns remain consistent. This should lead ultimately to propositions about non-experimental situations, but the problem is difficult and the solution is, as yet, in its infancy.

The third type of observation on our list is the simulation experiment, which is defined as any experiment on a system which is analogous, or intended to be analogous, to some other system about which the experimenter wishes to make some propositions. This would include both gaming and computer simulation. Further, we define as the *primary structure* or *primary system* (*referent system* is used by some writers), that in which one is interested but on which one cannot experiment (e.g. the international system); and the system on which experiments are being performed, as the *analogous* or *experimental structure* (or *system*).

While not the same, the problems involved in deriving information about the real world from simplified experiments and from simulations have a number of things in common. These are principally to do with obtaining the transference rules which enable propositions in the experimental situation, whatever its nature, to be taken over into the real world.

Simulation experiments are, in fact, widely used in the natural as well as the social sciences. A lot of knowledge about the human body or about, say, the effect of a drug on it is obtained through experiments on animals. On the definition here, such experiments are simulations. The bodies of animals like mice closely resemble those of humans, so a good deal of the information gained through experiments can be transferred to equivalent propositions about humans. Similarly, knowledge about the likely behaviour of new aircraft or ships is gained from the observation of models in wind tunnels or testing tanks. The simulations of the international system which we have been describing clearly fall into this category.

Implicit in the idea of simulations using human subjects is the notion that human groups have some common patterns of behaviour, even when these groups are drawn from very different backgrounds. Provisional tests of this, such as the study by Smoker on an extended version of the INS game, suggest that this is not unduly optimistic.

The above definition of simulation requires that we have criteria for deciding if and when the analogous structure behaves in the same way as the primary structure. Now this will not normally be exactly the case. Even scale models of things like aeroplanes do not behave in quite the same ways as the full-size version. In the murkier areas such as the simulation of behaviour, the discrepancies are much more significant. These take two forms. First, as a simulation is simpler than the primary structure, some factors present in the real world will not appear at all in the simulation. Secondly, many of the variables which appear in the simulation will move in ways different from those of the primary structure. This may not, in itself, be disturbing if the distortion of the variables is systematic, as we can still make propositions about the primary structure by applying the appropriate correction. Thus, supposing we have a simulation in which some variable always increases twice as fast as the equivalent variable in the primary structure; then, in order to discover what happens in reality, all that has to be done is to divide the appropriate simulation variable by two. Such simple transformations are unfortunately unlikely, but, in principle, much more sophisticated procedures can be applied.

We can define an *ideal simulation* as one which has the characteristic that it replicates some of the variables in the primary structure, where the deviations between the variables in the simulation and the primary structure are consistent (possibly in a statistical sense). All variables represented in the simulation should behave consistently with their analogues in the primary system. This last requirement arises because one purpose (prominent in the case of behavioural systems) of experimenting with a simulation is to examine the behaviour of variables which are hard to observe in the primary system. One example from a crisis game is the variation in tension as the crisis proceeds. It is possible to analyse this in real situations by such techniques as content analysis, and no doubt the increasing interest of psychologists in this sort of problem will lead to a more systematic study of written records from this point of view[36]. Nevertheless, the much closer range at which one can observe this in a simulation is of great advantage and permits more detailed analysis. Now, if we have a simulation in which all those aspects which are susceptible to check against real data behave consistently with those data, then it is legitimate to posit, or at least to hope, that those parts of the simulation which can only be checked by indirect methods are also behaving consistently with the variables in the primary system. However, if some behave consistently and some do not, then we have no particular reason for assuming that any one of the variables which is visible in the simulation but 'hidden' in the primary system is behaving consistently. The gaming simulation of an international system clearly falls very far short of the ideal. Not all aspects of behaviour are, at present, well reproduced, nor are we very sure which ones are well reproduced and which are not. Furthermore, the rules for transforming propositions about behaviour in gaming situations into ones about real situations are barely known. This does not mean, however, that simulations, even in their present stage, are useless. Even crude models can offer suggestions and stimulate insights. However one can not pretend that it is possible to test any propositions about the behaviour of real political systems.

Is it possible for gaming to develop into a more useful technique? The activity in a game depends on three factors. These are the personalities of the players, the structure of the game and, possibly, some chance element—a player might behave differently according to his physical and mental condition, the time of day, or any of the other factors which ensure that people are not completely predictable, even to those who know them well. It should be possible to learn enough about people playing in games to select subjects who are 'good gamers', where the criterion is that they should act like real decision-takers. The structure of the game is also something that can be experimented with until a combination of game structure and personality profiles of the players is found which tends to produce games which closely resemble in some respects actual political processes. If one were to get as far as this, then one would at least have a 'good simulation', even though it might fall short of the ideal. Whether or not this is possible is still an open question, though it is not an unreasonable hope. An 'ideal' simulation is further away, though in principle it is not impossible.

There is a crude criterion for determining whether one has achieved 'good simulation' of a crisis or, indeed, any system. Take some crisis which is little known, and run a number of games using this as a basis—that is, give people the history of the actual situation up to some selected point at the beginning of the crisis and let the game produce its own history from then on. Then write up the history of a number of these runs as if they were actual historical events, and also write up the true history in the same way. The histories can then be given to a number of accepted authorities on international behaviour, who are asked to pick out the genuine from the gaming histories. If they are unable to divide the games from reality with greater success than would be achieved by chance, then we conclude that the simulation was a 'good' one. It would be 'ideal' if we could generate in the game all the information which could have been observed in the real world, and if, having allowed the analysts to conduct any tests they wished (including such procedures as content analysis), they could still not distinguish between the real and the simulation histories. It may turn out that this is impossible, but it is a test which someone will carry out in the next few years, so a dogmatic assertion might prove embarrassing.

If we ever get to the stage where we have good or ideal simulations, we will have acquired an extremely powerful tool, which will necessitate a serious revision of the assertion that we cannot experiment with historical processes. If we could predict from appropriate personality tests who are going to be good gamers, we can put such people in games and see how they respond to other 'stooge players' who are acting, perhaps atypically, according to instructions. If a gamer reacts to international situations of a normal type as a real decision-maker does, then it is a plausible extrapolation to argue that he would also react to abnormal situations in a similar way. Thus we could begin to experiment with unusual types of foreign policy such as, say, unilateral nuclear disarmament of Britain, to see what would happen. While we would not have one hundred per cent confidence in the results, it would probably be a better prediction than any other—including the collective wisdom of the Foreign Office.

4 The Uses of Simulation

Simulation is a technique available for the analysis of the international system. However, 'analysis' has been used rather loosely, and we now need to examine more precisely the different functions which can be served by an analysis, the forms of analysis that the different functions imply, and the power of the technique in serving these functions.

We can distinguish four purposes for which simulation has been claimed to be an appropriate tool—education and training (between which a distinction will be drawn), hypothesis suggestion, hypothesis testing, and finally as a technique for revealing how different real life situations might develop.

a) *Training and education*

By training, we mean subjecting people who will, at some stage, be taking decisions in real life situations to an analogous gaming context to give them some feel of decision-taking. It is thereby hoped that they will be more effective when the time comes.

By education, we mean the use of a game to give someone whose purpose is to observe and analyse the situation, a greater understanding of it. These two purposes clearly overlap. Business games are commonly used for the first of these functions. If a game is sufficiently close to a real life situation, it helps the player understand the position of the executive and gives him practice in dealing with decision-making problems, without costing his firm thousands of pounds. At its strongest, the claim is that the players' situation really is close to real life. The problems to be solved are of an equivalent degree of complexity and the question of motivation (which is always brought up when these sort of exercises are discussed) is certainly solved in any high-powered American business school. At a weaker level, it can be argued that, even if the situation in the game is not equivalent to a real life problem, nevertheless the experience of solving a complex problem in a group under stress, and then of having to justify the solution before a critical audience, is itself an exercise of some importance. The argument is, in fact, that almost any complex problem would do. The common view is that the first and stronger position is legitimate. This is backed by the experience of business executives who have participated in such games and claim that there is sufficient congruence between real and gaming activities for it to be an effective training device.

As training devices, diplomatic games are not as far advanced as business games; as far as education is concerned, however, we can be less modest. A participant in a diplomatic game gets a totally different perspective of a problem by looking at it from one particular point of view as opposed to attempting to view it as a whole. A great deal of human conduct looks inexplicable, silly, or sometimes downright wicked, until one has looked at it from the inside. Some people make the necessary imaginative effort to put themselves in the position of a decision-taker with whom they have no intuitive sympathy, but very few. The discipline of the game, however, can excite the imagination to make the necessary leap. Even if, by participating in a game, nothing new is learned at a formal level, one appreciates emotionally many propositions which otherwise would have made no real impact on one's thinking; and one carries away a deeper appreciation of the situation than could have been acquired by any other process. Even the experienced analyst of international affairs can gain in emotional understanding from gaming, and possibly the cynicism (sometimes referred to as 'wisdom') which it seems necessary to acquire before becoming recognised as a reputable scholar of international relations might be modified or reduced, by participation in gaming.

b) *Hypothesis testing*

There is a growing number of hypotheses about behaviour in international systems and, in particular, crisis situations, which have been derived from games and tested in a gaming context.

The issue is whether such a procedure is legitimate. To what extent does the behaviour of subjects, who are, in practice, normally students, in an admittedly artificial situation, correspond to the behaviour of statesmen in real political situations? Do propositions about the one, necessarily carry over into the other context? We are undoubtedly testing hypotheses about students' behaviour in games, but to what extent we are testing propositions which are true of the other groups is by no means clear.

If there is a close correspondence between behaviour in gaming and in real situations, tests of hypotheses within a gaming context become provisional tests of the parallel hypotheses in real situations. They can, of course, be only provisional, having the same sort of status as the result of the test on a dog of some physiological theory which is intended to apply to a human being.

c) *Hypothesis suggestion*

A theory of behaviour in international systems must be based on hypotheses which are clearly formulated and operational, that is, testable. The problem is where to get the hypotheses from. One obvious possibility is the real world, but there are significant drawbacks to using this as the only source of hypotheses. Essentially these boil down to saying that we are able to observe an artificial structure at much closer quarters than a real structure, and thus to make observations from which we can derive hypotheses that would, to all intents and purposes, be unobservable in a real system.

This is, of course, not the only way in which hypotheses are generated within a gaming context. In a game, we can manipulate variables to see if they make any difference to the types of decision which are made. This may appear to be very close to using the game as a testing device. However, we are really trying to discover if a particular factor is significant, not what the actual result of altering it would be. This is testing, but in a weak form.

Let us take an example. Suppose we have a diplomatic game in which the teams consist of, say, Prime Minister, Minister of Finance and Chief of Staff. In one set of games we allow policy decisions to be taken as a result of free discussion between all members of the team, so that they are simple group decisions. In another set of games we allow free discussion between Prime

Minister and Minister of Finance, and between Prime Minister and Chief of Staff, but make communication between the Minister of Finance and the Chief of Staff difficult (this, of course, assumes that they are in separate rooms). The question is, would this make any difference to the type of decision which is made? There is some evidence, apart from that of our intuitions, that there would be significant differences. The experiments of Bevelas [47] and Leavitt [48] in a slightly different context imply that paths of communication are important factors in determining the types of decisions which a group will take. So, if differences do appear in the different sets of games, then this is *prima facie* evidence that communication patterns are variables which affect decisions. However, without much more detailed study of the technique of gaming, one would be very reluctant to suggest that the actual form of the differences observed in the game would also be paralleled in the real world. At the moment, at least, we have to be content with the weaker procedure.

This does, however, reveal two virtues of the gaming approach. First, it is possible to manipulate games in a way in which it is clearly impossible in the real world. Secondly, by posing a problem in a gaming framework and being faced with the problems of design, one's attention is drawn to certain variables which would otherwise be much less clearly perceived. Probably most historians would concede that communication patterns may be relevant to decision-taking, but the link between this and the work of psychologists on the same problem is not made. If all gaming does is to play the role of marriage broker between historians and psychologists, it will have achieved a great deal.

d) *Exploration of real life alternatives*

Games are sometimes played in which the scenario is based on a real life situation, such as in the Conex Middle Eastern game [49] or the Peace Research Centre's Viet Nam game [44]. The scenario must diverge at points from real life, but there is nevertheless an obvious relationship. Here we are concerned, not just with the alternative decision rules which are suggested, but with the whole history which is generated. We are, in fact, using the technique to suggest hypotheses about the system as a whole rather than about individual behaviour.

If we are concerned with a real situation and its future behaviour, then the game will give a set of possible directions for the future history. Some of these possibilities may be ones which a conventional analyst might have figured out for himself; some, however, may be new. The game involves a number of people thinking about the situation from different points of view in a way which the single analyst would be unlikely to achieve. A conventional analyst of a conflict situation is rather like a person playing chess against himself. Only unusual people can induce the requisite degree of temporary schizophrenia to make this seem like a genuine game.

In playing a game for the purpose of analysing a particular real situation, one loses nothing. The conventional analyst can look at a game history, reason it out in his own terms and decide on its inherent plausibility. If it is implausible, he can reject it, and if plausible, he can add it to his stockpile of possible future courses of development for the system under review. The worst that can happen is that the game will suggest no outcome that could not have been acquired by the other means available, and only time and a little money would have been lost.

In effect, one is using the game for prediction, but in a rather weak sense. The game outlines a number of possible directions for the system which might not have been appreciated without its assistance. It may miss what turns out to be the correct history but it adds to the range of contingencies which can be planned for. In the present state of the art, however, one can not say which of the many possible outcomes are the more probable. Even if we play the game a large enough number of times for one pattern to be the most probable in a statistically significant sense, this is still only a result about the game and cannot be regarded as a conclusion about the real world. It may be that such a transfer of conclusions will at some stage be possible, but this is not yet true —or rather, we do not know if it is true.

The types of problem on which simulation in its present form can throw some light are two. First, the technique can provide a pattern of decisions and events, the 'state' being viewed as the behavioural unit. Secondly, it is a technique for studying the various changes in perception which occur, particularly in crisis situations. In the experimental setting, the perceptual variables can be studied much more closely than is possible in real crisis situations, where the method of content analysis, though very valuable, is about the only formalised method available.

Simulations are, at present, rather weaker when it comes to variations in the decision-making process within the state. For instance, in crisis situations, the decision-making process alters, and stages which in less tense situations would be included, are missed out. In a simulation, however, people are given roles to play and, because the decision process is inherent in the design of the simulation, the process tends to remain the same.

In crisis games it is normal to fill only those roles which would be adopted in a crisis decision-making situation. However it is not, in principle, impossible to design a simulation which would be able to produce changes in the decision-making process itself, though it would be rather a large one.

chapter ten

Social Science and Values

1 Values and Policy Making

Social scientists make supposedly scientific statements about the behaviour of people in society. Their statements very frequently have great importance in the determination of policy. This is most obviously true in a discipline such as economics. The relevance of the study of conflict to policy is also very clear, though the discipline has not yet emerged with a sufficient body of tested and inter-related knowledge for it to be of much use in the formation of policy.

This raises some important questions. Can a social scientist, operating purely in his professional capacity, recommend one policy rather than another? Suppose a government is faced with a choice between two economic policies. Normally, of course, it faces a multitude of alternatives, but the principle of our argument is unaffected by this. A social scientist can examine both courses and see what their effects would be. If the actions were concerned with a thoroughly examined area of social life, then any two social scientists would agree on the consequences. Unfortunately, hardly any area is so unambiguously charted out. However, if the social scientists should disagree on how the world actually operates, then their disagreement is technical and they will attempt to settle it by technical and scientific argument and by the analysis of facts. Ideally, it should be possible for them to agree or to carry out some further research which would settle outstanding differences.

However, this description is of an ideal situation rather than of something which happens in practice very often—any more than it does in the natural sciences. It should not, however, obscure the distinction between scientific propositions which can, in principle, be settled by reference to facts, and value-questions implicit in the making of decisions which cannot be resolved in this way.

Here, we can distinguish between 'social science' and 'social engineering'. The former is a description of how social groups actually behave, and the second is a prescription for achieving specified goals in the light of the propositions discovered by the social scientists. The concept of a 'scientific' and an 'engineering' aspect of a discipline is common. The civil engineer, in building a bridge, makes use of the propositions of physics concerning the behaviour of materials under specified conditions—scientific propositions being utilised to alter the environment in some specified way. Similarly, medicine is the adjusting of the behaviour of the human body when, for some reason or other, it starts malfunctioning. This is done by reference to a large body of scientific theory and factual information about the operation of the human body, and its reaction to various inputs such as viruses and drugs. The more reliable the scientific information on which engineering is based, the more likely is engineering activity to achieve its intended aims.

Now, while in an advanced social science two social scientists might agree on their theoretical analysis of some particular problem and on what would be the most appropriate way to achieve the specified goal, there is no particular reason why they should agree that the goal is a desirable one. They may have different views on what the goals of the government should be, stemming from their respective visions of the 'Good Society'.

Once recommendations appear, values appear also, as to suggest one course of action rather than another is to imply that one state of the world is better than another. The scientist describes how the world behaves, the engineer shows how it could be altered, and then the decision-maker decides what is to be done. The last process obviously involves values. These, however, are already implicit at the engineering stage, in the assembling of the scientific information into a form suitable for making decisions.

We can illustrate the problem of the relationship between science and decision-taking in terms of a rather extreme example. Two sociologists might be in complete agreement that capital punishment would reduce the amount of sheep-stealing. One might recommend that capital punishment for the crime should not be instituted, believing that the sanctity of human life is more important than the reduction in the amount of sheep-stealing. The other might recommend that it be introduced, feeling that a strong line on the rights of property, and in particular of sheep owning, should be firmly asserted. They agree on that part of the problem which is within the province of social science, but differ radically on the values involved. Few people would accept the values implied by the second proposal today, but 150 years ago it was a widely held view, particularly amongst property owners.

There are many value-areas which are much more controversial today than the one illustrated. For example, there is disagreement concerning the responsibility of a firm for its employees. Should a business be constrained not to move out of a particular area because of the unemployment this would produce, even if it would be to the firm's advantage to go elsewhere?

Economists might be in agreement on the effects of the move, (and in such a case probably would achieve quite a high level of agreement). However, they divide into different groups over what they would recommend. Some would state that a firm should be allowed the freedom to act according to its own perceived interests. Others would maintain that it is proper to constrain it if its actions hurt other people who are unable to participate in the decision. This disagreement is not one of economics but of values, and, in this case, there is not general consensus on the relevant values as there is today in the sheep—stealing case.

The social sciences are not alone in being directly concerned with value decisions. Aspects of medicine also involve decisions which lie close to contested values. The concept of the healthy human being is less in dispute than that of the 'Good Society'. Nevertheless there are frequently many methods of curing a particular disease, each of which has its attendant advantages and disadvantages, and each of which may involve uncertainty. Strictly, the doctor's job is simply to tell the patient the consequences of the different possible courses of action and to let the patient make up his mind which he prefers. This is usually impracticable, however, and doctors frequently have to make authoritarian decisions, even when nominally giving a choice to the patient or his relatives. The concept of psychological health is much less clear cut than physical health. Not merely the means, but also the ends are in dispute, as in many of the social sciences.

The implication of this is that a social scientist should make clear his values, both to himself and to anyone to whom he makes a recommendation. All he is professionally competent to do is to analyse the effects of some policy. After that, his values are neither more nor less to be respected than those of other citizens. A government usually selects, as its senior advisers, people who agree at least broadly with its own values, so that there is less need for constant harping back to value-questions in the form 'If we want to achieve such and such, how do we go about it?' The social scientist is then put in the position of giving a technical answer to this problem, and his choice is either to answer it if he thinks the policy is morally proper, or to withdraw from the investigation if he does not.

The moral of this is that the social scientist must be careful not to let his values creep in surreptitiously under the guise of science. His analysis of social issues is of interest to the general public, but his values can claim no special hearing. The public, in their turn, should beware of the social scientist when he is making his recommendations. In saying that something is 'economically good' or 'sociologically desirable', he is making recommendations based on his own values and these should be recognised as such.

2 Values and Science

Decision making obviously involves values, as it involves the choice between alternatives, one of which is deemed better than the rest. Engineering implies values in that the act of working on a problem involves at least a limited approval of the value of the project. Science itself, however, is sometimes held to be value free. Two problems can easily get confused here. Scientific propositions in themselves are undoubtedly value free. Newton's laws of motion are accounts of how the world actually behaves, and carry with them no connotation either of approval or disapproval. However, the act of assert-ing a scientific statement is an action which may have consequences, and may therefore involve morality. The nature of the statement—whether it is logical, empirical, moral, aesthetic, or even whether it is correct or not—is irrelevant. Thus a discussion of Newton's (value-neutral) laws of motion with somebody who is about to drop a bomb is a moral action, as it will help him aim more effectively. For a physicist to talk to a bomber at such a time implies that he regards this particular piece of bombing as an appropriate thing to do, though this does not destroy the value-neutrality of the laws of motion themselves.

Not only the assertion of a set of scientific propositions, but also the initial decision to work on one line of investigation rather than another are actions which involve choices and hence morality. The decision of a social scientist to pursue one line of investigation rather than another implies that he believes that the line he is following is in some sense more important, though possibly from a personal rather than a social point of view.

It would be hard for a scientist to claim that, in choosing to work on the effects of toxic gases in the human body, he was not making a moral judgement if he knew that the results of his work were being used to increase the efficiency of the methods of killing Jews in concentration camps. However, moral problems are not always so clear cut. Work on the effect of certain viruses on the human body may be used for beneficial purposes in medicine, or for germ warfare. A scientist working in such an area is thus in a genuine moral dilemma, a dilemma in which social scientists also constantly find themselves, particularly if they are working on problems such as conflict, where the results of investigations might be used for a variety of widely different purposes. It is usually easier for the engineer to see the decision problems, and hence the moral problems, in his work. For the scientist, the moral problem is often by no means clear owing to the great uncertainty of the environment in which he operates.

One possible evasion is for a scientist to withdraw from the ethical dis-cussion and argue that he is trying to find the truth about the behaviour of nature and that the applications are other people's concern. This, however, is also a moral judgement in the sense that a refusal to make a moral judgement is itself a moral judgement.

Another area in which ethical issues can appear, at least in the short run, is the selection of the variables to be studied in relation to a particular problem, and the way in which these variables are treated. These choices are dictated by the scientist's present view of the world. As the social scientist can rarely abstract himself from his value-laden human condition, his choice is likely to correspond to his ideology.

In the long run, of course, the theories will be subject to test, and that which most successfully survives the tests will be preferred to the one which is most reassuring to the scientist. However, a proportion of the theories in the social sciencies at any given time are necessarily provisional, and are asserted partly because they conform to the preliminary assessment of the facts, and partly because they conform to the social scientist's values.

That there are moral problems involved in some scientific work is thus clear, and this is, perhaps, especially true in the social sciences, where research is often close to policy and decision. Scientific propositions are value-free, and a scientific argument is not an argument about values. However, it is not correct to conclude that the making of these propositions is not a moral act.

The confusion between the epistomelogical nature of scientific propositions (which are value-free) and the act of asserting the propositions (which does involve values) is at the heart of the problem of the supposed ethical neutrality of the social sciences.

3 Conclusion

The study of conflict as a social activity by the means of the methods of the social sciences is still in its relative infancy. Its findings are tentative, and applications to decision-making can be claimed for it only with diffidence. However, decisions have to be made, and it is better that they should be made on the basis of tested knowledge rather than of intuitive guesses. Admittedly, the use by governments of some of the theories which have been described in this book has not been such as to generate a great deal of confidence. The Theory of Games has been well digested in American strategic circles, but the consequences do not seem to have been very happy. This is not so much because the theory is wrong as because of its premature application to problems where both theory and data were inadequate, and where there were strong ideological predilections to accept certain interpretations and reject others. In this sort of situation, it is hardly surprising that the policies recommended did not turn out too well. However, the record of the intuitive analysts cannot bear much scrutiny either: the decisions on Suez and Czecho-slovakia were made without reference to the Theory of Games or any of the other scientific approaches to the study of behaviour.

Conflict Analysis is a primitive discipline. It is rather like medicine in its early stages when incorrect theories sometimes led to doctors doing more harm than good. However, by the nineteenth century, doctors with their still primitive scientific background probably did rather more good than would have been done by the application of traditional remedies based on a very selective observation of their past effects. The formalisation of the sciences did much to advance the reliability of their results. Similarly, the formalisation of the knowledge of human behaviour should, one day, enable society to contain and control violence, and thus to change and evolve rather less painfully than has been the case so far.

References

1 Washburn, S. L., 'Conflict in Primate Society' in de Reuck, Anthony and Knight, Julie (Eds), *Conflict in Society*, London, J. A. Churchill Ltd, 1966.
2 Burton, John W., *Conflict and Communication*, London, Macmillan, 1969.
3 Hobson, J. A., *Imperialism: A Study*, London, Allen and Unwin, 1938, 3rd Ed. (Revised). 1st Ed. 1902.
4 Lenin, *Imperialism: The Final Stage of Capitalism*, 1st published 1917. English Edition, London, Lawrence and Wishart, 1939.
5 Wright, Quincy, *A Study of War*, 2 vols., Chicago, Chicago University Press, 1947.
6 Richardson, L. F., *Arms and Insecurity*, London, Stevens and Sons, 1960.
7 Richardson, L. F., *Statistics of Deadly Quarrels*, London, Stevens and Sons, 1960.
8 Richardson, L. F., *Weather Prediction by Numerical Process,* London, Cambridge University Press, 1922.
9 Cyert, R. M. and March, J. G., *A Behavioural Theory of the Firm*, Englewood Cliffs, N.J., Prentice-Hall, 1963.
10 Montagu, Ashley, *Men and Aggression*, London, Oxford University Press, 1968.
11 Brown, J. A. C., *Freud and the Post-Freudians*, Harmondsworth. Penguin, 1961.
12 Jones, Earnest, *Sigmund Freud* (3 vols), New York, Basic Books, 1955.
13 Galtung, Johan, 'A Structural Theory of Aggression', *Journal of Peace Research*, 1964, No. 2.
14 Schlesinger, Arthur M., *A Thousand Days: John F. Kennedy in the White House*, London, Deutsch, 1965.
15 Sorensen, Theodore C., *Kennedy*, London, Macmillan, 1965
16 Taylor, A. J. P., *English History* 1914-45, Oxford, Oxford University Press, 1965.
17 Rummell, R. J., 'Understanding Factor Analysis', *Journal of Conflict Resolution*, Vol. XI, No. 4, 1967. This article has a useful bibliography.
18 Tantner, Raymond, 'Dimensions of Conflict Behaviour within and between Nations, 1958-60', *Journal of Conflict Resolution*, Vol. X, No. 1, 1966.
19 Von Neumann, John, and Morgenstern, Oscar, *The Theory of Games and Economic Behaviour*, Princeton, Princeton University Press, 1953. (Second Ed.).
20 Schelling, Thomas C., *The Strategy of Conflict*, Cambridge, Mass, Harvard University Press, 1960.
21 Luce, Duncan and Raiffa, Howard, *Games and Decisions*, New York, John Wiley, 1957.
22 Rapoport A., and Chammah A. M., *Prisoner's Dilemma: A Study of Conflict and Cooperation*, Ann Arbor, University of Michigan Press, 1965.
23 Nash, J. F., 'The Bargaining Problem', *Econometrica* 18, 1950.
24 Rapoport, A., *Two Person Game Theory*, Ann Arbor, University of Michigan Press, 1966.

25 Coddington, Alan, *Theories of the Bargaining Process*, London, Allen and Unwin Ltd, 1968.

26 Cross, J. G., 'A Theory of the Bargaining Process', *American Economic Review* 55, 1965.

27 Nicholson, Michael, 'Tariff Wars and a Model of Conflict', *Journal of Peace Research*, 1967, No. 1.

28 Kaplan, Morton, *System and Process in International Politics*, New York, John Wiley and Sons, 1957. Discusses different forms of alliance system.

29 A much more detailed discussion of this sort of issue, largely in terms of domestic political coalitions, is contained in Riker, William H., *The Theory of Political Coalitions*, New Haven, Yale University Press, 1962.

30 Stone, Richard, 'The Theory of Games', *Economic Journal*, LVIII, 1968.

31 Horvath, William J., and Foster, Caxton C., 'Stochastic Models of War Alliances', *General Systems*, VIII, 1963.

32 Singer, J. David, and Small, Melvin, 'Alliance Aggregation and the Onset of War 1815-1945' in Singer, J. David (Ed.), *Quantitative International Politics*, New York, The Free Press, 1968.

33 Popper, Karl, 'Prediction and Prophecy in the Social Sciences' in *Conjectures and Refutations*, London, Routledge and Kegan Paul, 1963.

34 Deutsch, Karl, W., *The Nerves of Government*, New York, The Free Press, 1963.

35 Vital, David, *The Making of British Foreign Policy*, London, Allen and Unwin, 1968.

36 North, Robert C., Holsti, Ole R., Zaninovich, M. George, and Zinnes, Dina A., *Content Analysis: A Handbook with Application for the Study of International Crisis*, Evanston, Illinois, North-Western University Press, 1963.

37 A well-known treatment in traditional style is Bull, Hedley, *The Control of the Arms Race*, London, Weidenfeld and Nicolson, 1961.

38 Smoker, Paul, 'A Mathematical Study of the Present Arms Race', and 'A Pilot Study of the Present Arms Race', both in *General Systems*, VIII, 1963.

39 Fouraker, Lawrence, and Siegel, Sidney, *Bargaining Behaviour*, New York, McGraw-Hill, 1963.

40 Wilson, Andrew, *The Bomb and the Computer*, London, Barrie and Rockliff, 1968, for a very readable account of a number of simulations.

41 Raser, John, *Simulation and Society: an examination of scientific gaming*, Boston (Mass), Allyn and Bacon, 1969.

42 Dill, W. R., et al., 'Experiences in a Complex Management Game', *California Management Review*, Spring 1961. Reprinted as Graduate School of Industrial Administration Reprint Series, No. 74, Carnegie-Mellon University.

43 Guetzkow, Harold, et al., *Simulation in International Relations: Developments for Research and Teaching*, Englewood Cliffs, N. J., Prentice-Hall, 1963.

44 MacRae, John, and Smoker, Paul, 'A Vietnam Simulation', *Journal of Peace Research*, No. 1, 1967.

45 Hermann, Charles, and Hermann, Margaret, 'An Attempt to Simulate the Outbreak of World War I', *American Political Science Review*, 61, 1967.

46 de Sola Pool, Ithiel, and Kessler, A., 'The Kaiser, the Czar and the Computer: Information Processing in a Crisis', *American Behavioural Scientist*, Vol. VIII, No. 9, 1965.

47 Bevelas, A., 'Communication Patterns in Task Oriented Groups' in Lerner, O., and Lasswell, H. D. (Eds), *The Policy Sciences*, Stamford, 1951.

48 Leavitt, H. J., 'The Effects of Certain Communication Patterns on Group Performance', *Journal of Abnormal and Social Psychology*, 1951.

49 Banks, Michael H., Groom, A. J. R., and Oppenheim, A. N., 'Gaming and Simulation in International Relations', *Political Studies*, Vol. XVI, No. 1, 1968.

Index